4th Watch Books™

Forward

Our purpose for publishing the documents issued by the National Institute of Standards and Technology (NIST) is twofold. First of all, each NIST title in and of itself is very informative, however I am of the opinion that they should be looked at from the standpoint that each title is an integral part of a holistic cybersecurity strategy. Rather than look at each title just by itself, we need to look at them in groups based on how they are interrelated and designed to work together to improve cybersecurity.

For example, this particular group on FORENSICS security includes the following titles:

NIST SP 800-61 R 2   Computer Security Incident Handling Guide

NIST SP 800-72   Guidelines on PDA Forensics

NIST SP 800-83   Guide to Malware Incident Prevention and Handling for Desktops and Laptops

NIST SP 800-86   Guide to Integrating Forensic Techniques into Incident Response

NIST SP 800-88 R1   Guidelines for Media Sanitization

NIST SP 800-184   Guide for Cybersecurity Event Recovery

In order to assemble the entire picture of Forensics security – from what it is, how it works, what the vulnerabilities are and how to mitigate them, one must examine all of these documents. Only by going through all of them can a person understand the complete picture. Leave one of them out and you would be missing a valuable piece of the Forensics security puzzle.

Why buy a book you can download for free?

That brings me to the second reason to publish the NIST standards and that is the logistics of it all. These 7 publications consist of 771 pages. That's enough paper to fill two large three-ring binders. Nobody has a secretary anymore, so an engineer that is paid $75 an hour has to do this. The amount of time it would take an engineer to print all 7 publications (using a network printer shared with 100 other people – and it's out of paper, and the toner is low), punch holes in 771 pages and assemble the binders would easily take half a day. Our ability to deliver any NIST document quickly and efficiently is unmatched because we are printing books on demand and we are backed up by Amazon, so the titles are easy to find and simple to order. Just search Amazon.com by NIST number and you can have a copy shipped to you in a matter of days. We print all books a full 8 ½ inches by 11 inches, with large text. If there are color images in the publication, the book is probably in color, unless the color is merely decorative, in which case we print in black and white to keep the cost to you as low as possible.

Luis Ayala,
My email is cybah@webplus.net Our website is: cybah.webplus.net
4th Watch Books is a Service Disabled Veteran Owned Small Business (SDVOSB).

Following is an excerpt from the book titled "**Cyber-Physical Attack Defenses: Preventing Damage to Buildings and Utilities**", by Luis Ayala. Available at Amazon.com, Barnes & Noble and Books-a-Million.

Hacking into a Building Controls Systems (BCS), Industrial Controls Systems (ICS), and Supervisory Controls and Data Acquisition (SCADA) networks is not the same as breaking into enterprise networks that process information. BCS, ICS and SCADA systems are much more complex. Breaking into a controls system is only a means to an end. The target is not the network itself, it is the equipment being controlled.

A cyber-physical attack represents a weaponization of the Internet.

Although designing a catastrophic cyber-physical attack scenario to exploit a particular physical process requires a solid engineering background and in-depth destructive knowledge of the target controls system (Cyber-Physical Attack Engineering) – you don't need an engineering background to figure out how to turn equipment off.

In addition, a typical ICS contains multiple control loops and sometimes the control loops are nested and/or cascading, so the set point for one loop is based on the process variable output from another loop. Interrupting one process can have a ripple effect through the factory. Supervisory control loops and lower-level loops operate continuously over the duration of a process with cycle times of milliseconds.

A cracker doesn't need to have an engineering degree to figure out that a large change in the setpoint (or process values) on a proportional feedback system will have a larger effect than a small change that would be tolerated based on the sensitivity of the control system and the process. But, even a small change that results in sluggish response in the short-term could have a major effect over a relatively long period of time.

The only saving grace is that a newbie or script kiddie will not thoroughly understand complex manufacturing processes. While a newbie may be able to turn off the lights in the factory, I doubt he would know how to increase the deadband (an interval of a signal domain where no action occurs - the system is 'dead' - i.e. the output is zero) on voltage regulators, or cause repeated activation-deactivation cycles.

Hacking a chemical plant to create a weapon of mass destruction (a Bhopal-style catastrophic failure) for example, requires knowledge of physics, chemistry and engineering, as well as a great deal about how the network is laid out, and a keen understanding of process-aware defensive systems. The most a newbie could hope to do is to turn something off.

A well-qualified attacker (such as a foreign security service) hitting a building or utilities controls network seeks to take control over the equipment. Those crackers understand the equipment they will be controlling. No offense but, most IT guys are not familiar with electrical and mechanical equipment, industrial and manufacturing equipment, or utility equipment, so they wouldn't know how to defend them. That's because they don't know the equipment or processes being controlled.

The same is true of the folks in charge of physical security at these facilities. The typical security guys don't know anything about electrical and mechanical systems, or how computer networks are designed. Let's face it, they don't have the budget or the training to deal with these new threats.

The owner is looking to the facility guys, the IT guys and the security guys to work together to defend their physical plant, and in many cases, these guys aren't even talking to each other. Most of the time, they think cyber-physical security is someone else's responsibility! In essence, "nobody is minding the store". An effective defense against cyber-physical attacks requires procedural safeguards, such as frequent password changes, equipment inspections, random drills, security awareness programs, records retention programs, etc.

So, what is the big deal?

On December 3 1984, in Bhopal, India there was an industrial accident at a pesticide plant that immediately killed at least 3,800 people and caused significant morbidity and premature death for many thousands more. That was only one incident with a release of only 40 tons of methyl isocyanate gas. Of course, this was an accident and not a cyber-physical attack, but it should give you an idea what could happen in a worst-case scenario.

Imagine you wake up in the morning and go the bathroom. You turn on the faucet and nothing happens. You go back to the bedroom and the clock is flashing 12:00. You hit the power button on the TV remote and nothing happens. It's a little warm in the house but the air conditioning doesn't work. Then you realize that though the sun is out and it's a normal weekday, you don't hear any cars going by. You go outside to your car and it won't start – even the radio doesn't work. The cell phone has no signal and won't stay on when you power up. The toaster doesn't heat up and you have to light the gas stove with a match. It's a nice day so you walk to work and notice a line outside the supermarket, but the doors are locked. You ask why they don't open up and they say there is no power to run the cash registers. Even their backup generator won't start. None of the traffic lights work, but there are no cars on the road anyway. This is a cyber-physical attack that affects all utilities, and many electronic devices.

Or, imagine you've been waiting for months to find a kidney donor and the day you go in for a kidney transplant, the hospital is attacked and the refrigeration equipment that holds human organs is hacked. A malicious attacker changed the temperature setting of the refrigerators overnight, or cut the power entirely. All human organs were lost. Yes, these systems are designed with alarms that send messages to beepers and email, but a determined attacker can defeat those alarms.

Another example is what actually happened at a Chrysler assembly plant. An attacker shut down one auto plant with a worm that quickly spread to all other Chrysler plants, idling 50,000 workers. These were professionally-installed industrial control networks with firewalls and safety features. I suspect they were protected in much the same way that many enterprise networks are protected today.

The bad news is that crackers are getting better at what they do. In the good old days, an attacker would use a virus or worm to take over your computer. Nowadays they can attack your computer without loading any files at all. That's because all the files they need to take over are already loaded on your computer. That's called a Fileless Cyber-Attack. All they need to do is trick you into giving them permission to access those files. Anti-virus software has gotten very good at detecting and stopping a computer virus. Attackers find it much easier to fool a human using social engineering.

In order for you to begin to understand what is going through the mind of someone trying to break into your computer network, I include a lot of Hackerspeak, or Leet-speak in this book. See the definitions a little further on. This should give you some insight into the mind of a hacker.

This book was written to help Owners, Architects, Engineers, and facilities and infrastructure maintenance personnel understand the vulnerability of SCADA systems, building controls systems, and industrial controls systems to cyber-physical attack. The book includes simple descriptions of the vulnerabilities (attack vectors) of automated equipment controls common to buildings, industry and utilities. The book also lists the different types of cyber-physical attacks discovered. It is a handy desk reference for Architects, Engineers, Building Managers, Students, Researchers and Consultants interested in preventing cyber-physical attacks. Remember, a "hacker" and a "cracker" are two different meanings so please stop referring to hackers as bad guys.

The price of connectivity is less security. The more connected a device is, the less secure it will be.

7. Monitor the Process Equipment Looking for Anomalies

It is probably easier to detect a cyber-physical attack (when it occurs) by looking at how the equipment is operating than it is to detect subtle software anomalies or dropped packets. Although boiler water temperature and pressure rising dangerous levels doesn't necessarily signal that a cyber-physical attack is underway, it could be an attack. Don't assume it isn't a cyber-attack out of hand. Look for signs that the controls have been manipulated. Compare what the computer says is happening with what the equipment is actually doing. Remember, a sneaky attacker will change the setpoints higher than normal so the computer will not know something is wrong.

Malicious attackers are more likely to use the process control systems to make equipment "misbehave" while appearing to operate normally. At the Iranian nuclear plant, Stuxnet manipulated the calibration systems so the plant workers didn't see the real pressure readings that would have flagged the problems with the devices early on. Had the workers manually checked the equipment itself frequently, they would have noticed the discrepancy.

A malicious attacker would schedule his attack when it would be less likely to be detected or when it could do the most damage. Startup and shutdown of a process plant are the two most dangerous operational modes of the plant. A well-qualified attacker would know the planned startup sequence of operations and manipulate the amount of heat or the flow of chemicals to corrupt the process and damage the hardware.

For example, industrial distillation is typically performed in large, vertical cylindrical columns known as distillation towers or distillation columns. The amount of heat entering a distillation column is a crucial operating parameter, addition of excess or insufficient heat to the column can lead to foaming, weeping, entrainment, or flooding. If the column contains liquid during pressuring, excessive vapor flows will cause flooding and gas lifting of the liquid, resulting in liquid discharge into relief header and damage the column internals.

The information in this NIST title directly addresses the concerns I articulated in my Cyber-Physical Attack Defenses book. By implementing the attached standard, hopefully your system can survive an attempted cyber-physical attack.

Luis Ayala

NIST Special Publication 800-39

Managing Information Security Risk

Organization, Mission, and Information System View

National Institute of Standards and Technology

U.S. Department of Commerce

JOINT TASK FORCE
TRANSFORMATION INITIATIVE

INFORMATION SECURITY

Computer Security Division
Information Technology Laboratory
National Institute of Standards and Technology
Gaithersburg, MD 20899-8930

March 2011

U.S. Department of Commerce
Gary Locke, Secretary

National Institute of Standards and Technology
Patrick D. Gallagher, Director

Reports on Computer Systems Technology

The Information Technology Laboratory (ITL) at the National Institute of Standards and Technology (NIST) promotes the U.S. economy and public welfare by providing technical leadership for the nation's measurement and standards infrastructure. ITL develops tests, test methods, reference data, proof of concept implementations, and technical analyses to advance the development and productive use of information technology. ITL's responsibilities include the development of management, administrative, technical, and physical standards and guidelines for the cost-effective security and privacy of other than national security-related information in federal information systems. The Special Publication 800-series reports on ITL's research, guidelines, and outreach efforts in information system security, and its collaborative activities with industry, government, and academic organizations.

Authority

This publication has been developed by NIST to further its statutory responsibilities under the Federal Information Security Management Act (FISMA), Public Law (P.L.) 107-347. NIST is responsible for developing information security standards and guidelines, including minimum requirements for federal information systems, but such standards and guidelines shall not apply to national security systems without the express approval of appropriate federal officials exercising policy authority over such systems. This guideline is consistent with the requirements of the Office of Management and Budget (OMB) Circular A-130, Section 8b(3), *Securing Agency Information Systems*, as analyzed in Circular A-130, Appendix IV: *Analysis of Key Sections*. Supplemental information is provided in Circular A-130, Appendix III, *Security of Federal Automated Information Resources*.

Nothing in this publication should be taken to contradict the standards and guidelines made mandatory and binding on federal agencies by the Secretary of Commerce under statutory authority. Nor should these guidelines be interpreted as altering or superseding the existing authorities of the Secretary of Commerce, Director of the OMB, or any other federal official. This publication may be used by nongovernmental organizations on a voluntary basis and is not subject to copyright in the United States. Attribution would, however, be appreciated by NIST.

NIST Special Publication 800-39, 88 pages

(March 2011)

National Institute of Standards and Technology
Attn: Computer Security Division, Information Technology Laboratory
100 Bureau Drive (Mail Stop 8930) Gaithersburg, MD 20899-8930
Electronic mail: sec-cert@nist.gov

Compliance with NIST Standards and Guidelines

In accordance with the provisions of FISMA,[1] the Secretary of Commerce shall, on the basis of standards and guidelines developed by NIST, prescribe standards and guidelines pertaining to federal information systems. The Secretary shall make standards compulsory and binding to the extent determined necessary by the Secretary to improve the efficiency of operation or security of federal information systems. Standards prescribed shall include information security standards that provide minimum information security requirements and are otherwise necessary to improve the security of federal information and information systems.

- Federal Information Processing Standards (FIPS) are approved by the Secretary of Commerce and issued by NIST in accordance with FISMA. FIPS are compulsory and binding for federal agencies.[2] FISMA requires that federal agencies comply with these standards, and therefore, agencies may not waive their use.

- Special Publications (SPs) are developed and issued by NIST as recommendations and guidance documents. For other than national security programs and systems, federal agencies must follow those NIST Special Publications mandated in a Federal Information Processing Standard. FIPS 200 mandates the use of Special Publication 800-53, as amended. In addition, OMB policies (including OMB Reporting Instructions for FISMA and Agency Privacy Management) state that for other than national security programs and systems, federal agencies must follow certain specific NIST Special Publications.[3]

- Other security-related publications, including interagency reports (NISTIRs) and ITL Bulletins, provide technical and other information about NIST's activities. These publications are mandatory only when specified by OMB.

- Compliance schedules for NIST security standards and guidelines are established by OMB in policies, directives, or memoranda (e.g., annual FISMA Reporting Guidance).[4]

---

[1] The E-Government Act (P.L. 107-347) recognizes the importance of information security to the economic and national security interests of the United States. Title III of the E-Government Act, entitled the Federal Information Security Management Act (FISMA), emphasizes the need for organizations to develop, document, and implement an organization-wide program to provide security for the information systems that support its operations and assets.

[2] The term *agency* is used in this publication in lieu of the more general term *organization* only in those circumstances where its usage is directly related to other source documents such as federal legislation or policy.

[3] While federal agencies are required to follow certain specific NIST Special Publications in accordance with OMB policy, there is flexibility in how agencies apply the guidance. Federal agencies apply the security concepts and principles articulated in the NIST Special Publications in accordance with and in the context of the agency's missions, business functions, and environment of operation. Consequently, the application of NIST guidance by federal agencies can result in different security solutions that are equally acceptable, compliant with the guidance, and meet the OMB definition of *adequate security* for federal information systems. Given the high priority of information sharing and transparency within the federal government, agencies also consider reciprocity in developing their information security solutions. When assessing federal agency compliance with NIST Special Publications, Inspectors General, evaluators, auditors, and assessors consider the intent of the security concepts and principles articulated within the specific guidance document and how the agency applied the guidance in the context of its mission/business responsibilities, operational environment, and unique organizational conditions.

[4] Unless otherwise stated, all references to NIST publications in this document (i.e., Federal Information Processing Standards and Special Publications) are to the most recent version of the publication.

Acknowledgements

This publication was developed by the *Joint Task Force Transformation Initiative* Interagency Working Group with representatives from the Civil, Defense, and Intelligence Communities in an ongoing effort to produce a unified information security framework for the federal government. The National Institute of Standards and Technology wishes to acknowledge and thank the senior leaders from the Departments of Commerce and Defense, the Office of the Director of National Intelligence, the Committee on National Security Systems, and the members of the interagency technical working group whose dedicated efforts contributed significantly to the publication. The senior leaders, interagency working group members, and their organizational affiliations include:

U.S. Department of Defense

Teresa M. Takai
Assistant Secretary of Defense for Networks and Information Integration/DoD Chief Information Officer (Acting)

Gus Guissanie
Deputy Assistant Secretary of Defense (Acting)

Dominic Cussatt
Senior Policy Advisor

Barbara Fleming
Senior Policy Advisor

Office of the Director of National Intelligence

Adolpho Tarasiuk Jr.
Assistant Director of National Intelligence and Intelligence Community Chief Information Officer

Charlene P. Leubecker
Deputy Intelligence Community Chief Information Officer

Mark J. Morrison
Director, Intelligence Community Information Assurance

Roger Caslow
Chief, Risk Management and Information Security Programs Division

National Institute of Standards and Technology

Cita M. Furlani
Director, Information Technology Laboratory

William C. Barker
Cyber Security Advisor, Information Technology Laboratory

Donna Dodson
Chief, Computer Security Division

Ron Ross
FISMA Implementation Project Leader

Committee on National Security Systems

Teresa M. Takai
Acting Chair, CNSS

Eustace D. King
CNSS Subcommittee Co-Chair

Peter Gouldmann
CNSS Subcommittee Co-Chair

Lance Dubsky
CNSS Subcommittee Co-Chair

Joint Task Force Transformation Initiative Interagency Working Group

Ron Ross
NIST, JTF Leader

Gary Stoneburner
Johns Hopkins APL

Jennifer Fabius-Greene
The MITRE Corporation

Kelley Dempsey
NIST

Deborah Bodeau
The MITRE Corporation

Cheri Caddy
Intelligence Community

Peter Gouldmann
Department of State

Arnold Johnson
NIST

Peter Williams
Booz Allen Hamilton

Karen Quigg
The MITRE Corporation

Richard Graubart
The MITRE Corporation

Christian Enloe
NIST

In addition to the above acknowledgments, a special note of thanks goes to Peggy Himes and Elizabeth Lennon for their superb technical editing and administrative support and to Bennett Hodge, Cassandra Kelly, Marshall Abrams, Marianne Swanson, Patricia Toth, Kevin Stine, and Matt Scholl for their valuable insights and contributions. The authors also gratefully acknowledge and appreciate the significant contributions from individuals and organizations in the public and private sectors, both nationally and internationally, whose thoughtful and constructive comments improved the overall quality, thoroughness, and usefulness of this publication.

DEVELOPING COMMON INFORMATION SECURITY FOUNDATIONS

COLLABORATION AMONG PUBLIC AND PRIVATE SECTOR ENTITIES

In developing standards and guidelines required by FISMA, NIST consults with other federal agencies and offices as well as the private sector to improve information security, avoid unnecessary and costly duplication of effort, and ensure that NIST publications are complementary with the standards and guidelines employed for the protection of national security systems. In addition to its comprehensive public review and vetting process, NIST is collaborating with the Office of the Director of National Intelligence (ODNI), the Department of Defense (DoD), and the Committee on National Security Systems (CNSS) to establish a common foundation for information security across the federal government. A common foundation for information security will provide the Intelligence, Defense, and Civil sectors of the federal government and their contractors, more uniform and consistent ways to manage the risk to organizational operations and assets, individuals, other organizations, and the Nation that results from the operation and use of information systems. A common foundation for information security will also provide a strong basis for reciprocal acceptance of security assessment results and facilitate information sharing. NIST is also working with public and private sector entities to establish mappings and relationships between the security standards and guidelines developed by NIST and the International Organization for Standardization (ISO) and International Electrotechnical Commission (IEC).

CAUTIONARY NOTE

INTENDED SCOPE AND USE OF THIS PUBLICATION

The guidance provided in this publication is intended to address *only* the management of information security-related risk derived from or associated with the operation and use of information systems or the environments in which those systems operate. The guidance is *not* intended to replace or subsume other risk-related activities, programs, processes, or approaches that organizations have implemented or intend to implement addressing areas of risk management covered by other legislation, directives, policies, programmatic initiatives, or mission/business requirements. Rather, the information security risk management guidance described herein is complementary to and should be used as part of a more comprehensive Enterprise Risk Management (ERM) program.

Table of Contents

Prologue

"... Through the process of risk management, leaders must consider risk to U.S. interests from adversaries using cyberspace to their advantage and from our own efforts to employ the global nature of cyberspace to achieve objectives in military, intelligence, and business operations..."

"... For operational plans development, the combination of threats, vulnerabilities, and impacts must be evaluated in order to identify important trends and decide where effort should be applied to eliminate or reduce threat capabilities; eliminate or reduce vulnerabilities; and assess, coordinate, and deconflict all cyberspace operations..."

"... Leaders at all levels are accountable for ensuring readiness and security to the same degree as in any other domain..."

-- THE NATIONAL STRATEGY FOR CYBERSPACE OPERATIONS
OFFICE OF THE CHAIRMAN, JOINT CHIEFS OF STAFF, U.S. DEPARTMENT OF DEFENSE

CHAPTER ONE

INTRODUCTION

THE NEED FOR INTEGRATED ORGANIZATION-WIDE RISK MANAGEMENT

Information technology is widely recognized as the engine that drives the U.S. economy, giving industry a competitive advantage in global markets, enabling the federal government to provide better services to its citizens, and facilitating greater productivity as a nation. Organizations[5] in the public and private sectors depend on technology-intensive *information systems*[6] to successfully carry out their missions and business functions. Information systems can include diverse entities ranging from high-end supercomputers, workstations, personal computers, cellular telephones, and personal digital assistants to very specialized systems (e.g., weapons systems, telecommunications systems, industrial/process control systems, and environmental control systems). Information systems are subject to serious *threats* that can have adverse effects on organizational operations (i.e., missions, functions, image, or reputation), organizational assets, individuals, other organizations, and the Nation by exploiting both known and unknown vulnerabilities to compromise the confidentiality, integrity, or availability of the information being processed, stored, or transmitted by those systems. Threats to information and information systems can include purposeful attacks, environmental disruptions, and human/machine errors and result in great harm to the national and economic security interests of the United States. Therefore, it is imperative that leaders and managers at all levels understand their responsibilities and are held accountable for managing information security risk—that is, the risk associated with the operation and use of information systems that support the missions and business functions of their organizations.

Organizational risk can include many types of risk (e.g., program management risk, investment risk, budgetary risk, legal liability risk, safety risk, inventory risk, supply chain risk, and security risk). Security risk related to the operation and use of information systems is just one of many components of organizational risk that senior leaders/executives address as part of their ongoing risk management responsibilities. Effective risk management requires that organizations operate in highly complex, interconnected environments using state-of-the-art and legacy information systems—systems that organizations depend on to accomplish their missions and to conduct important business-related functions. Leaders must recognize that explicit, well-informed risk-based decisions are necessary in order to balance the benefits gained from the operation and use of these information systems with the risk of the same systems being vehicles through which purposeful attacks, environmental disruptions, or human errors cause mission or business failure. Managing information security risk, like risk management in general, is not an exact science. It brings together the best collective judgments of individuals and groups within organizations responsible for strategic planning, oversight, management, and day-to-day operations—providing both the necessary and sufficient risk response measures to adequately protect the missions and business functions of those organizations.

---

[5] The term *organization* describes an entity of any size, complexity, or positioning within an organizational structure (e.g., a federal agency or, as appropriate, any of its operational elements) that is charged with carrying out assigned mission/business processes and that uses information systems in support of those processes.

[6] An *information system* is a discrete set of information resources organized for the collection, processing, maintenance, use, sharing, dissemination, or disposition of information. In the context of this publication, the definition includes the environment in which the information system operates (i.e., people, processes, technologies, facilities, and cyberspace).

The complex relationships among missions, mission/business processes, and the information systems supporting those missions/processes require an integrated, organization-wide view for managing risk.[7] Unless otherwise stated, references to *risk* in this publication refer to information security risk from the operation and use of organizational information systems including the processes, procedures, and structures within organizations that influence or affect the design, development, implementation, and ongoing operation of those systems. The role of information security in managing risk from the operation and use of information systems is also critical to the success of organizations in achieving their strategic goals and objectives. Historically, senior leaders/executives have had a very narrow view of information security either as a technical matter or in a stovepipe that was independent of organizational risk and the traditional management and life cycle processes. This extremely limited perspective often resulted in inadequate consideration of how information security risk, like other organizational risks, affects the likelihood of organizations successfully carrying out their missions and business functions. This publication places information security into the broader organizational context of achieving mission/business success. The objective is to:

- Ensure that senior leaders/executives recognize the importance of managing information security risk and establish appropriate *governance* structures for managing such risk;

- Ensure that the organization's risk management process is being effectively conducted across the three tiers of organization, mission/business processes, and information systems;

- Foster an organizational climate where information security risk is considered within the context of the design of mission/business processes, the definition of an overarching enterprise architecture, and system development life cycle processes; and

- Help individuals with responsibilities for information system implementation or operation better understand how information security risk associated with their systems translates into organization-wide risk that may ultimately affect the mission/business success.

To successfully execute organizational missions and business functions with information system-dependent processes, senior leaders/executives must be committed to making risk management a fundamental mission/business requirement. This top-level, executive commitment ensures that sufficient resources are available to develop and implement effective, organization-wide risk management programs. Understanding and addressing risk is a *strategic* capability and an *enabler* of missions and business functions across organizations. Effectively managing information security risk organization-wide requires the following key elements:

- Assignment of risk management responsibilities to senior leaders/executives;

- Ongoing recognition and understanding by senior leaders/executives of the information security risks to organizational operations and assets, individuals, other organizations, and the Nation arising from the operation and use of information systems;

- Establishing the organizational tolerance for risk and communicating the risk tolerance throughout the organization including guidance on how risk tolerance impacts ongoing decision-making activities;[8] and

- Accountability by senior leaders/executives for their risk management decisions and for the implementation of effective, organization-wide risk management programs.

---

[7] The aggregation of different types of risk across the organization is beyond the scope of this publication.

[8] The evaluation of *residual risk* (which changes over time) to determine acceptable risk is dependent on the threshold set by organizational *risk tolerance*.

1.1 PURPOSE AND APPLICABILITY

NIST Special Publication 800-39 is the flagship document in the series of information security standards and guidelines developed by NIST in response to FISMA. The purpose of Special Publication 800-39 is to provide guidance for an integrated, organization-wide program for managing information security risk to organizational operations (i.e., mission, functions, image, and reputation), organizational assets, individuals, other organizations, and the Nation resulting from the operation and use of federal information systems. Special Publication 800-39 provides a structured, yet flexible approach for managing risk that is intentionally broad-based, with the specific details of assessing, responding to, and monitoring risk on an ongoing basis provided by other supporting NIST security standards and guidelines. The guidance provided in this publication is not intended to replace or subsume other risk-related activities, programs, processes, or approaches that organizations have implemented or intend to implement addressing areas of risk management covered by other legislation, directives, policies, programmatic initiatives, or mission/business requirements. Rather, the risk management guidance described herein is complementary to and should be used as part of a more comprehensive Enterprise Risk Management (ERM) program.

This publication satisfies the requirements of FISMA and meets or exceeds the information security requirements established for executive agencies[9] by the Office of Management and Budget (OMB) in Circular A-130, Appendix III, *Security of Federal Automated Information Resources.* The guidelines in this publication are applicable to all federal information systems other than those systems designated as national security systems as defined in 44 U.S.C., Section 3542. The guidelines have been broadly developed from a technical perspective to complement similar guidelines for national security systems and may be used for such systems with the approval of appropriate federal officials exercising policy authority over such systems. State, local, and tribal governments, as well as private sector organizations are encouraged to consider using these guidelines, as appropriate.

1.2 TARGET AUDIENCE

This publication is intended to serve a diverse group of risk management professionals including:

- Individuals with oversight responsibilities for risk management (e.g., heads of agencies, chief executive officers, chief operating officers);

- Individuals with responsibilities for conducting organizational missions/business functions (e.g., mission/business owners, information owners/stewards, authorizing officials);

- Individuals with responsibilities for acquiring information technology products, services, or information systems (e.g., acquisition officials, procurement officers, contracting officers);

- Individuals with information security oversight, management, and operational responsibilities (e.g., chief information officers, senior information security officers,[10] information security managers, information system owners, common control providers);

---

[9] An *executive agency* is: (i) an executive department specified in 5 U.S.C., Section 101; (ii) a military department specified in 5 U.S.C., Section 102; (iii) an independent establishment as defined in 5 U.S.C., Section 104(1); and (iv) a wholly owned government corporation fully subject to the provisions of 31 U.S.C., Chapter 91. In this publication, the term *executive agency* is synonymous with the term *federal agency*.

[10] At the *agency* level, this position is known as the Senior Agency Information Security Officer. Organizations may also refer to this position as the *Chief Information Security Officer*.

- Individuals with information system/security design, development and implementation responsibilities (e.g., program managers, enterprise architects, information security architects, information system/security engineers; information systems integrators); and

- Individuals with information security assessment and monitoring responsibilities (e.g., system evaluators, penetration testers, security control assessors, independent verifiers/validators, inspectors general, auditors).

1.3 RELATED PUBLICATIONS

The risk management approach described in this publication is supported by a series of security standards and guidelines necessary for managing information security risk. In particular, the Special Publications developed by the Joint Task Force Transformation Initiative[11] supporting the unified information security framework for the federal government include:

- Special Publication 800-37, *Guide for Applying the Risk Management Framework to Federal Information Systems: A Security Life Cycle Approach*;

- Special Publication 800-53, *Recommended Security Controls for Federal Information Systems and Organizations*;

- Special Publication 800-53A, *Guide for Assessing the Security Controls in Federal Information Systems and Organizations*; and

- Draft Special Publication 800-30, *Guide for Conducting Risk Assessments*.[12]

In addition to the Joint Task Force publications listed above, the International Organization for Standardization (ISO) and the International Electrotechnical Commission (IEC) publish standards for risk management and information security including:

- ISO/IEC 31000, *Risk management – Principles and guidelines*;

- ISO/IEC 31010, *Risk management – Risk assessment techniques*;

- ISO/IEC 27001, *Information technology – Security techniques – Information security management systems – Requirements*; and

- ISO/IEC 27005, *Information technology – Security techniques – Information security risk management systems*.

NIST's mission includes harmonization of international and national standards where appropriate. The concepts and principles contained in this publication are intended to implement for federal information systems and organizations, an information security management system and a risk management process similar to those described in ISO/IEC standards. This reduces the burden on organizations that must conform to both ISO/IEC standards and NIST standards and guidance.

---

[11] An overview of each Joint Task Force Transformation Initiative publication, similar to an Executive Summary, can be obtained through appropriate NIST ITL Security Bulletins at http://csrc.nist.gov.

[12] Special Publication 800-39 supersedes the original Special Publication 800-30 as the source for guidance on risk management. Special Publication 800-30 is being revised to provide guidance on risk assessment as a supporting document to Special Publication 800-39.

1.4 ORGANIZATION OF THIS SPECIAL PUBLICATION

The remainder of this special publication is organized as follows:

- **Chapter Two** describes: (i) the components of risk management; (ii) the multitiered risk management approach; (iii) risk management at the organization level (Tier 1); (iv) risk management at the mission/business process level (Tier 2); (v) risk management at the information system level (Tier 3); (vi) risk related to trust and trustworthiness; (vii) the effects of organizational culture on risk; and (viii) relationships among key risk management concepts.

- **Chapter Three** describes a life cycle-based process for managing information security risk including: (i) a general overview of the risk management process; (ii) how organizations establish the context for risk-based decisions; (iii) how organizations assess risk; (iv) how organizations respond to risk; and (v) how organizations monitor risk over time.

- **Supporting appendices** provide additional risk management information including: (i) general references; (ii) definitions and terms; (iii) acronyms; (iv) roles and responsibilities; (v) risk management process tasks; (vi) governance models; (vii) trust models; and (viii) risk response strategies.

CHAPTER TWO

THE FUNDAMENTALS

BASIC CONCEPTS ASSOCIATED WITH RISK MANAGEMENT

This chapter describes the fundamental concepts associated with managing information security risk across an organization including: (i) the components of risk management; (ii) the multitiered risk management approach; (iii) risk management at Tier 1 (organization level); (iv) risk management at Tier 2 (mission/business process level); (v) risk management at Tier 3 (information system level); (vi) risk related to trust and trustworthiness; (vii) the effects of organizational culture on risk; and (viii) the relationships among key risk management concepts.

2.1 COMPONENTS OF RISK MANAGEMENT

Managing risk is a complex, multifaceted activity that requires the involvement of the entire organization—from senior leaders/executives providing the strategic vision and top-level goals and objectives for the organization; to mid-level leaders planning, executing, and managing projects; to individuals on the front lines operating the information systems supporting the organization's missions/business functions. Risk management is a comprehensive process that requires organizations to: (i) *frame* risk (i.e., establish the context for risk-based decisions); (ii) *assess* risk; (iii) *respond* to risk once determined; and (iv) *monitor* risk on an ongoing basis using effective organizational communications and a feedback loop for continuous improvement in the risk-related activities of organizations. Risk management is carried out as a holistic, organization-wide activity that addresses risk from the strategic level to the tactical level, ensuring that risk-based decision making is integrated into every aspect of the organization.[13] The following sections briefly describe each of the four risk management components.

The first component of risk management addresses how organizations *frame* risk or establish a risk context—that is, describing the environment in which risk-based decisions are made. The purpose of the risk framing component is to produce a *risk management strategy* that addresses how organizations intend to assess risk, respond to risk, and monitor risk—making explicit and transparent the risk perceptions that organizations routinely use in making both investment and operational decisions. The risk frame establishes a foundation for managing risk and delineates the boundaries for risk-based decisions within organizations. Establishing a realistic and credible risk frame requires that organizations identify: (i) risk assumptions (e.g., assumptions about the threats, vulnerabilities, consequences/impact, and likelihood of occurrence that affect how risk is assessed, responded to, and monitored over time); (ii) risk constraints (e.g., constraints on the risk assessment, response, and monitoring alternatives under consideration); (iii) risk tolerance (e.g., levels of risk, types of risk, and degree of risk uncertainty that are acceptable); and (iv) priorities and trade-offs (e.g., the relative importance of missions/business functions, trade-offs among different types of risk that organizations face, time frames in which organizations must address risk, and any factors of uncertainty that organizations consider in risk responses). The risk framing component and the associated risk management strategy also include any strategic-level decisions on how risk to organizational operations and assets, individuals, other organizations, and the Nation, is to be managed by senior leaders/executives.

---

[13] Integrated, enterprise-wide risk management includes, for example, consideration of: (i) the strategic goals/objectives of organizations; (ii) organizational missions/business functions prioritized as needed; (iii) mission/business processes; (iv) enterprise and information security architectures; and (v) system development life cycle processes.

The second component of risk management addresses how organizations *assess* risk within the context of the organizational risk frame. The purpose of the risk assessment component is to identify: (i) threats to organizations (i.e., operations, assets, or individuals) or threats directed through organizations against other organizations or the Nation; (ii) vulnerabilities internal and external to organizations;[14] (iii) the harm (i.e., consequences/impact) to organizations that may occur given the potential for threats exploiting vulnerabilities; and (iv) the likelihood that harm will occur. The end result is a determination of risk (i.e., the degree of harm and likelihood of harm occurring). To support the risk assessment component, organizations identify: (i) the tools, techniques, and methodologies that are used to assess risk; (ii) the assumptions related to risk assessments; (iii) the constraints that may affect risk assessments; (iv) roles and responsibilities; (v) how risk assessment information is collected, processed, and communicated throughout organizations; (vi) how risk assessments are conducted within organizations; (vii) the frequency of risk assessments; and (viii) how threat information is obtained (i.e., sources and methods).

The third component of risk management addresses how organizations *respond* to risk once that risk is determined based on the results of risk assessments. The purpose of the risk response component is to provide a consistent, organization-wide, response to risk in accordance with the organizational risk frame by: (i) developing alternative courses of action for responding to risk; (ii) evaluating the alternative courses of action; (iii) determining appropriate courses of action consistent with organizational risk tolerance; and (iv) implementing risk responses based on selected courses of action. To support the risk response component, organizations describe the types of risk responses that can be implemented (i.e., accepting, avoiding, mitigating, sharing, or transferring risk). Organizations also identify the tools, techniques, and methodologies used to develop courses of action for responding to risk, how courses of action are evaluated, and how risk responses are communicated across organizations and as appropriate, to external entities (e.g., external service providers, supply chain partners).[15]

The fourth component of risk management addresses how organizations *monitor* risk over time. The purpose of the risk monitoring component is to: (i) verify that planned risk response measures are implemented and information security requirements derived from/traceable to organizational missions/business functions, federal legislation, directives, regulations, policies, and standards, and guidelines, are satisfied; (ii) determine the ongoing effectiveness of risk response measures following implementation; and (iii) identify risk-impacting changes to organizational information systems and the environments in which the systems operate.[16] To support the risk monitoring component, organizations describe how compliance is verified and how the ongoing effectiveness of risk responses is determined (e.g., the types of tools, techniques, and methodologies used to determine the sufficiency/correctness of risk responses and if risk mitigation measures are implemented correctly, operating as intended, and producing the desired effect with regard to reducing risk). In addition, organizations describe how changes that may impact the ongoing effectiveness of risk responses are monitored.

---

[14] Organizational vulnerabilities are not confined to information systems but can include, for example, vulnerabilities in governance structures, mission/business processes, enterprise architecture, information security architecture, facilities, equipment, system development life cycle processes, supply chain activities, and external service providers.

[15] Supply chain risk management guidance is provided in NIST Interagency Report 7622.

[16] Environments of operation include, but are not limited to: the threat space; vulnerabilities; missions/business functions; mission/business processes; enterprise and information security architectures; information technologies; personnel; facilities; supply chain relationships; organizational governance/culture; procurement/acquisition processes; organizational policies/procedures; organizational assumptions, constraints, risk tolerance, and priorities/trade-offs.

As indicated in the four components of risk management described above, organizations also consider external risk relationships, as appropriate. Organizations identify external entities with which there is an actual or potential risk relationship (i.e., organizations which could impose risks on, transfer risks to, or communicate risks to other organizations, as well as those to which organizations could impose, transfer, or communicate risks). External risk relationships include, for example, suppliers, customers or served populations, mission/business partners, and/or service providers. For organizations dealing with advanced persistent threats (i.e., a long-term pattern of targeted, sophisticated attacks) the risk posed by external partners (especially suppliers in the supply chain) may become more pronounced. Organizations establish practices for sharing risk-related information (e.g., threat and vulnerability information) with external entities, including those with which the organizations have a risk relationship as well as those which could supply or receive risk-related information (e.g., Information Sharing and Analysis Centers [ISAC], Computer Emergency Response Teams [CERT]).

Figure 1 illustrates the risk management process and the information and communications flows among components. The black arrows represent the *primary* flows within the risk management process with risk *framing* informing all the sequential step-by-step set of activities moving from risk *assessment* to risk *response* to risk *monitoring*. For example, one of the primary outputs from the risk framing component is a description of the sources and methods that organizations use in acquiring threat information (e.g., open source, classified intelligence community reports). The output regarding threat information is a primary input to the risk assessment component and is communicated accordingly to that component. Another example is illustrated in the primary output from the risk assessment component—that is, a determination of risk. The output from the risk assessment component is communicated to the risk response component and is received as a primary input for that component. Another primary input to the risk response component is an output from the risk framing component—the risk management strategy that defines how the organization should respond to risk. Together, these inputs, along with any additional inputs, are used by decision makers when selecting among potential courses of action for risk responses.

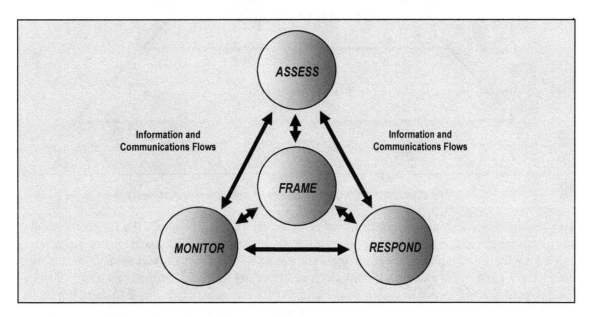

FIGURE 1: RISK MANAGEMENT PROCESS

The bidirectional nature of the arrows indicates that the information and communication flows among the risk management components as well as the execution order of the components, may be flexible and respond to the dynamic nature of the risk management process. For example, new legislation, directives, or policies may require that organizations implement additional risk response measures immediately. This information is communicated directly from the risk framing component to the risk response component where specific activities are carried out to achieve compliance with the new legislation, directives, or policies, illustrating the very dynamic and flexible nature of information as it moves through the risk management process. Chapter Three provides a complete description of the organization-wide risk management process including specifications for inputs/preconditions, activities, and outputs/post conditions.

2.2 MULTITIERED RISK MANAGEMENT

To integrate the risk management process throughout the organization, a three-tiered approach is employed that addresses risk at the: (i) *organization* level; (ii) *mission/business process* level; and (iii) *information system* level. The risk management process is carried out seamlessly across the three tiers with the overall objective of continuous improvement in the organization's risk-related activities and effective inter-tier and intra-tier communication among all stakeholders having a shared interest in the mission/business success of the organization. Figure 2 illustrates the three-tiered approach to risk management along with some of its key characteristics.

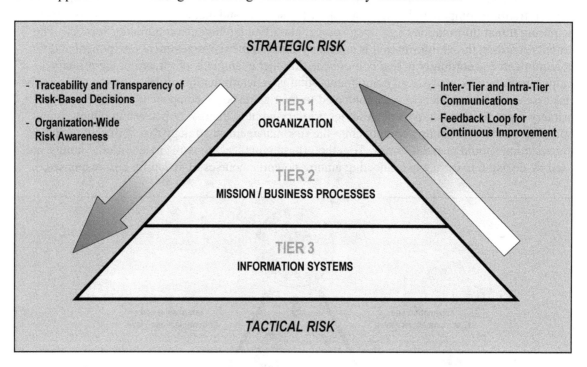

FIGURE 2: MULTITIERED ORGANIZATION-WIDE RISK MANAGEMENT

Tier 1 addresses risk from an *organizational* perspective. Tier 1 implements the first component of risk management (i.e., risk framing), providing the context for all risk management activities carried out by organizations. Tier 1 risk management activities directly affect the activities carried out at Tiers 2 and 3. For example, the missions and business functions defined at Tier 1 influence the design and development of the mission/business processes created at Tier 2 to carry out those missions/business functions. Tier 1 provides a prioritization of missions/business functions which in turn drives investment strategies and funding decisions, thus, affecting the development of enterprise architecture (including embedded information security architecture) at Tier 2 and the allocations and deployment of management, operational, and technical security controls at Tier 3.

Other examples of Tier 1 activities that affect Tier 2 and Tier 3 activities include the selection of common controls, the provision of guidance from the risk executive (function)[17] to authorizing officials, and the establishment of the order of recovery for information systems supporting critical missions and business operations. Section 2.3 provides a more detailed description of the specific activities associated with Tier 1.

Tier 2 addresses risk from a *mission/business process* perspective and is informed by the risk context, risk decisions, and risk activities at Tier 1. Tier 2 risk management activities include: (i) defining the mission/business processes needed to support the missions and business functions of organizations; (ii) prioritizing the mission/business processes with respect to the strategic goals and objectives of organizations; (iii) defining the types of information needed to successfully execute the mission/business processes, the criticality/sensitivity of the information, and the information flows both internal and external to organizations; (iv) incorporating information security requirements[18] into the mission/business processes; and (v) establishing an enterprise architecture[19] with embedded information security architecture[20] that promotes cost-effective and efficient information technology solutions consistent with the strategic goals and objectives of the organization and measures of performance. Tier 2 activities directly affect the activities carried out at Tier 3. For example, the information security architecture portion of the enterprise architecture developed at Tier 2 influences and guides the allocation of information protection needs which, in turn, influences and guides the allocation of the security controls to specific components of organizational information systems at Tier 3. Enterprise architecture decisions at Tier 2 affect the design of information systems at Tier 3 including the types of information technologies acceptable for use in developing those systems. The activities carried out at Tier 2 can also provide useful feedback to Tier 1, possibly resulting in revisions to the organizational risk frame or affecting risk management activities carried out at Tier 1, for example those performed by the risk executive (function). Section 2.4 provides a more detailed description of the specific activities associated with Tier 2.

Tier 3 addresses risk from an *information system* perspective and is guided by the risk context, risk decisions and risk activities at Tiers 1 and 2. Tier 3 risk management activities include: (i) categorizing organizational information systems; (ii) allocating security controls to organizational information systems and the environments in which those systems operate consistent with the organization's established enterprise architecture and embedded information security architecture; and (iii) managing the selection, implementation, assessment, authorization, and ongoing monitoring of allocated security controls as part of a disciplined and structured system development life cycle process implemented across the organization. At Tier 3, information system owners, common control providers, system and security engineers, and information system security officers make risk-based decisions regarding the implementation, operation, and

---

[17] The risk executive (function) is described in Section 2.3.2.

[18] Information security requirements can be obtained from a variety of sources (e.g., legislation, policies, directives, regulations, standards, and organizational mission/business/operational requirements). Organization-level security requirements are documented in the information security program plan or equivalent document.

[19] Federal Enterprise Architecture Reference Models and Segment and Solution Architectures are defined in the OMB Federal Enterprise Architecture (FEA) Program, *FEA Consolidated Reference Model Document,* Version 2.3, October 2003, and OMB *Federal Segment Architecture Methodology (FSAM),* January 2009, respectively.

[20] The *information security architecture* describes the security-related aspects of the enterprise architecture that are incorporated into the enterprise architecture definition as an integral part of the architecture development—that is a sub-architecture derived from the enterprise architecture, not a separately defined layer or architecture.

monitoring of organizational information systems. Based on these day-to-day operational risk-based decisions, authorizing officials make follow-on risk-based decisions on whether or not the information systems are initially authorized to operate within the designated environments of operation or continue to receive authorization to operate on an ongoing basis. These ongoing risk-based decisions are informed by the risk management process with guidance from the risk executive (function) and the various architectural considerations supporting the mission/business processes. In addition, the activities at Tier 3 provide essential feedback to Tiers 1 and 2. New vulnerabilities discovered in an organizational information system, for example, may have systemic implications that extend organization-wide. Those same vulnerabilities may trigger changes to the enterprise architecture and embedded information security architecture or may require an adjustment to the organizational risk tolerance. Section 2.5 provides a more detailed description of the specific activities associated with Tier 3.

> *Since mission and business success in organizations depends on information systems, those systems must be dependable. To be dependable in the face of sophisticated threats, the information systems must be used wisely in accordance with the degree of protection and resilience achieved.*

2.3 TIER ONE—ORGANIZATION VIEW

Tier 1 addresses risk from an *organizational* perspective by establishing and implementing *governance* structures that are consistent with the strategic goals and objectives of organizations and the requirements defined by federal laws, directives, policies, regulations, standards, and missions/business functions. Governance structures provide oversight for the risk management activities conducted by organizations and include: (i) the establishment and implementation of a *risk executive (function)*; (ii) the establishment of the organization's risk management strategy including the determination of *risk tolerance*; and (iii) the development and execution of organization-wide *investment strategies* for information resources and information security.

2.3.1 Governance

In general, *governance* is the set of responsibilities and practices exercised by those responsible for an organization (e.g., the board of directors and executive management in a corporation, the head of a federal agency) with the express goal of: (i) providing strategic direction; (ii) ensuring that organizational mission and business objectives are achieved; (iii) ascertaining that risks are managed appropriately; and (iv) verifying that the organization's resources are used responsibly.[21] Risks and resources can be associated with different organizational sectors (e.g., legal, finance, information technology, regulatory compliance, information security). Different sectors require specialized expertise in order to manage the risks associated with that sector. Thus, governance within organizations frequently is organized by sector.[22] The five outcomes of governance related to organization-wide risk management are:

---

[21] This definition is adapted from the IT Governance Institute. The Chartered Institute of Management Accountants and the International Federation of Accountants also adopted this definition in 2004.

[22] While governance is frequently organized by sectors, organizations are well served by establishing a single aligned governance approach. A unified governance approach can coordinate the individual sector governance activities and provide a consistent governance approach, organization-wide.

- Strategic alignment of risk management decisions with missions and business functions consistent with organizational goals and objectives;

- Execution of risk management processes to frame, assess, respond to, and monitor risk to organizational operations and assets, individuals, other organizations, and the Nation;

- Effective and efficient allocation of risk management resources;

- Performance-based outcomes by measuring, monitoring, and reporting risk management metrics to ensure that organizational goals and objectives are achieved; and

- Delivered value by optimizing risk management investments in support of organizational objectives.[23]

As part of organizational governance, senior leaders/executives in consultation and collaboration with the risk executive (function), determine: (i) the types of risk management decisions that are reserved for specific senior leadership roles (e.g., heads of agencies or chief executive officers, chief financial officers, chief information officers, chief information security officers);[24] (ii) the types of risk management decisions that are deemed to be organization-wide and the types of decisions that can be delegated to subordinate organizations or to other roles in the organization (e.g., systems and security engineers, mission/business owners, enterprise architects, information security architects, common infrastructure or service providers, authorizing officials); and (iii) how risk management decisions will be communicated to and by the risk executive (function). Three different types of governance models (i.e., centralized, decentralized, and hybrid) are described in Appendix F. Regardless of the governance model(s) employed, clear assignment and accountability for accepting risk is essential for effective risk management.

> *Strong governance is the best indicator of senior leadership commitment to effective, consistent risk management across the organization to achieve ongoing mission/business success.*

2.3.2 Risk Executive (Function)

The risk executive is a functional role established within organizations to provide a more comprehensive, organization-wide approach to risk management. The *risk executive (function)* serves as the common risk management resource for senior leaders/executives, mission/business owners, chief information officers, chief information security officers, information system owners, common control providers,[25] enterprise architects, information security architects, information systems/security engineers, information system security managers/officers, and any other stakeholders having a vested interest in the mission/business success of organizations. The risk executive (function) coordinates with senior leaders/executives to:

- Establish risk management roles and responsibilities;

---

[23] Information security governance outcomes adapted from *IT Governance Institute, Information Security Governance: Guidance for Boards of Directors and Executive Management*, 2nd Edition, 2006.

[24] There is no implication by listing various titles within an organization of any particular relationship (peer or otherwise) or lines of authority.

[25] A *common control provider* is an organizational official responsible for the development, implementation, assessment, and monitoring of common controls (i.e., security controls inherited by information systems).

- Develop and implement an organization-wide *risk management strategy* that guides and informs organizational risk decisions (including how risk is framed, assessed, responded to, and monitored over time); [26]

- Manage threat and vulnerability information with regard to organizational information systems and the environments in which the systems operate;

- Establish organization-wide forums to consider all types and sources of risk (including aggregated risk);

- Determine organizational risk based on the aggregated risk from the operation and use of information systems and the respective environments of operation;

- Provide oversight for the risk management activities carried out by organizations to ensure consistent and effective risk-based decisions;

- Develop a greater understanding of risk with regard to the strategic view of organizations and their integrated operations;

- Establish effective vehicles and serve as a focal point for communicating and sharing risk-related information among key stakeholders internally and externally to organizations;

- Specify the degree of autonomy for subordinate organizations permitted by parent organizations with regard to framing, assessing, responding to, and monitoring risk; [27]

- Promote cooperation and collaboration among authorizing officials to include security authorization actions requiring shared responsibility (e.g., joint/leveraged authorizations); [28]

- Ensure that security authorization decisions consider all factors necessary for mission and business success; and

- Ensure shared responsibility for supporting organizational missions and business functions using external providers receives the needed visibility and is elevated to appropriate decision-making authorities.

The risk executive (function) presumes neither a specific organizational structure nor formal responsibility assigned to any one individual or group within the organization. Heads of agencies or organizations may choose to retain the risk executive (function) or to delegate the function. The risk executive (function) requires a mix of skills, expertise, and perspectives to understand the strategic goals and objectives of organizations, organizational missions/business functions, technical possibilities and constraints, and key mandates and guidance that shape organizational operations. To provide this needed mixture, the risk executive (function) can be filled by a single individual or office (supported by an expert staff) or by a designated group (e.g., a risk board,

---

[26] Organizational risk decisions include investment decisions (see Section 2.3.4). Organizational *risk tolerance* is determined as part of the risk framing component (see Section 2.3.3) and defined in the risk management strategy.

[27] Because subordinate organizations responsible for carrying out derivative or related missions may have already invested in their own methods of framing, assessing, responding to, and monitoring risk, parent organizations may allow a greater degree of autonomy within parts of the organization or across the entire organization in order to minimize costs. When a diversity of risk management activities is allowed, organizations may choose to employ, when feasible, some means of translation and/or synthesis of the risk-related information produced from those activities to ensure that the output of the different activities can be correlated in a meaningful manner.

[28] NIST Special Publication 800-37 provides guidance on joint and leveraged authorizations.

executive steering committee, executive leadership council).[29] The risk executive (function) fits into the organizational governance structure in such a way as to facilitate efficiency and to maximize effectiveness. While the organization-wide scope situates the risk executive (function) at Tier 1, its role entails ongoing communications with and oversight of the risk management activities of mission/business owners, authorizing officials, information system owners, common control providers, chief information officers, chief information security officers, information system and security engineers, information system security managers/officers, and other stakeholders at Tiers 2 and 3.

> *To be effective, organization-wide risk management programs require the strong commitment, direct involvement, and ongoing support from senior leaders/executives. The objective is to institutionalize risk management into the day-to-day operations of organizations as a priority and an integral part of how organizations conduct operations in cyberspace—recognizing that this is essential in order to successfully carry out missions in threat-laden operational environments.*

2.3.3 Risk Management Strategy

An organizational *risk management strategy*, one of the key outputs of risk framing, addresses how organizations intend to assess, respond to, and monitor risk—the risk associated with the operation and use of organizational information systems. The risk management strategy makes explicit the specific assumptions, constraints, risk tolerances, and priorities/trade-offs used within organizations for making investment and operational decisions. The risk management strategy also includes any strategic-level decisions and considerations on how senior leaders/executives are to manage information security risk to organizational operations and assets, individuals, other organizations, and the Nation. An organization-wide risk management strategy includes, for example, an unambiguous expression of the risk tolerance for the organization, acceptable risk assessment methodologies, risk response strategies, a process for consistently evaluating risk across the organization with respect to the organization's risk tolerance, and approaches for monitoring risk over time. The use of a risk executive (function) can facilitate consistent, organization-wide application of the risk management strategy. The organization-wide risk management strategy can be informed by risk-related inputs from other sources both internal and external to the organization to ensure the strategy is both broad-based and comprehensive.

An important Tier 1 risk management activity and also part of risk framing, is the determination of *risk tolerance*. Risk tolerance is the level of risk or degree of uncertainty that is acceptable to organizations and is a key element of the organizational risk frame. Risk tolerance affects all components of the risk management process—having a direct impact on the risk management decisions made by senior leaders/executives throughout the organization and providing important constraints on those decisions. For example, risk tolerance affects the nature and extent of risk management oversight implemented in organizations, the extent and rigor of risk assessments performed, and the content of organizational strategies for responding to risk. With regard to risk assessments, more risk-tolerant organizations may be concerned only with those threats that peer organizations have experienced while less risk-tolerant organizations may expand the list to include those threats that are theoretically possible, but which have not been observed in operational environments. With regard to risk response, less risk-tolerant organizations are likely

---

[29] Organizations emphasize the need for inclusiveness within the risk executive (function) by senior leaders/executives in mission/business areas to help ensure proper information security planning, resourcing, and risk management.

to require additional grounds for confidence in the effectiveness of selected safeguards and countermeasures or prefer safeguards and countermeasures that are more mature and have a proven track record. Such organizations may also decide to employ multiple safeguards and countermeasures from multiple sources (e.g., antivirus software at clients and servers that are provided by different vendors). Another example illustrating the impact of risk tolerance on risk response is that risk tolerance can also affect the organizational requirements for trustworthiness provided by specific information technologies. Two organizations may choose the same information technologies, but their relative degree of risk tolerance may impact the degree of assessment required prior to deployment.

There is no correct level of organizational risk tolerance. Rather, the degree of risk tolerance is: (i) generally indicative of organizational culture; (ii) potentially different for different types of losses/compromises; and (iii) highly influenced by the individual subjective risk tolerance of senior leaders/executives. Yet, the ramifications of risk decisions based on risk tolerance are potentially profound, with less risk-tolerant organizations perhaps failing to achieve needed mission/business capabilities in order to avoid what appears to be unacceptable risk; while more risk-tolerant organizations may focus on near-term mission/business efficiencies at the expense of setting themselves up for future failure. It is important that organizations exercise due diligence in determining risk tolerance—recognizing how fundamental this decision is to the effectiveness of the risk management program.

2.3.4 Investment Strategies

Investment strategies[30] play a significant role in organizational risk management efforts. These strategies generally reflect the long-term strategic goals and objectives of organizations and the associated risk management strategies developed and executed to ensure mission and business success. Underlying all investment strategies is the recognition that there is a finite amount of resources available to invest in helping organizations effectively manage risk—that is, effectively addressing risk to achieve on-going mission/business success.

Mission and Risk Priorities

Organizations generally conduct a variety of missions and are involved in different types of business functions. This is especially true for large and complex organizations that have different organizational components, each of which is typically focused on one or two primary missions. While all of these organizational components and associated missions/business functions are likely to be important and play a key role in the overall success of organizations, in reality they are not of equal importance. The greater the criticality of organizational missions and business functions, the greater the necessity for organizations to ensure that risks are adequately managed. Such missions and business functions are likely to require a greater degree of risk management investments than missions/business functions deemed less critical. The determination of the relative importance of the missions/business functions and hence the level of risk management investment, is something that is decided upon at Tier 1, executed at Tier 2, and influences risk management activities at Tier 3.

Anticipated Risk Response Needs

There is a great variation in the nature of potential threats facing organizations, ranging from hackers attempting to merely deface organizational Web sites (e.g., cyber vandalism), to insider

---

[30] Investment strategies can include organizational approaches to: (i) replacing legacy information systems (e.g., phasing items in gradually, replacing entirely); (ii) outsourcing and using external providers of information systems and services; and (iii) internal development vs. acquisition of commercially available information technology products.

threats, to sophisticated terrorist groups/organized criminal enterprises seeking to exfiltrate sensitive information, to a nation state's military attempting to destroy or disrupt critical missions by attacking organizational information systems.[31] The strategic investments required to address the risk from more traditional adversaries (e.g., hackers conducting small-group activities with limited capabilities) are considerably different than the investments required to address the risk associated with advanced persistent threats consistent with more advanced adversaries (e.g., nation states or terrorist groups with highly sophisticated levels of expertise and resources that seek to establish permanent footholds in organizations for purposes of impeding aspects of the organizational missions). To address less sophisticated threats, organizations can focus their efforts at Tier 3—investing to ensure that needed safeguards and countermeasures (e.g., security controls, security services, and technologies) are obtained, implemented correctly, operating as intended, and producing the desired effect with regard to meeting information security policies and addressing known vulnerabilities. In addition to these basic investments, organizations can also invest in continuous monitoring processes to ensure that the acquired security controls, services, and technologies are operating effectively throughout the system development life cycle.

When organizations need to address advanced persistent threats, it is likely that adequately addressing related risks at Tier 3 is not feasible because necessary security solutions are not currently available in the commercial marketplace. In those instances, organizations must purposefully invest beyond Tier 3 for significant response capabilities at Tier 2, and to some extent at Tier 1. At Tier 3, the nature of investment is likely to change from implementation of existing solutions to an added strategic focus on investing in leading-edge information security technologies (essentially experimenting with innovative security solutions/technologies and being an early adopter) or investing in information security research and development efforts to address specific technology gaps.[32] Information security investments to address advanced persistent threats may require expenditures over the course of several years, as new security solutions and technologies transition from research to development to full deployment. The long-term view of strategic investing in the risk response needs for organizations can help to reduce the continuing focus on near-term vulnerabilities discovered in information systems—vulnerabilities that exist due to the complexity of the information technology products and systems and the inherent weaknesses in those products and systems.

Limitations on Strategic Investments

The ability of organizations to provide strategic information security investments is limited. Where the desired strategic investment funding or strategic resources[33] are not available to address specific needs, organizations may be forced to make compromises. For example, organizations might extend the time frame required for strategic information security objectives to be accomplished. Alternatively, organizations might prioritize risk management investments, opting to provide resources (financial or otherwise) to address some critical strategic needs sooner than other less critical needs. All investment decisions require organizations to prioritize risks and to assess the potential impacts associated with alternative courses of action.

---

[31] The threats described above are a subset of the overarching threat space that also includes errors of omission and commission, natural disasters, and accidents.

[32] This investment strategy is a change from vulnerability and patch management to a longer-term strategy addressing information security gaps such as the lack of information technology products with the trustworthiness necessary to achieve information system resilience in the face of advanced persistent threats.

[33] In some instances, the limitations may not be financial in nature, but limitations in the number of individuals with the appropriate skills/expertise or limitations regarding the state of technology.

2.4 TIER TWO—MISSION/BUSINESS PROCESS VIEW

Tier 2 addresses risk from a *mission/business process* perspective by designing, developing, and implementing mission/business processes that support the missions/business functions defined at Tier 1. Organizational mission/business processes guide and inform the development of an enterprise architecture that provides a disciplined and structured methodology for managing the complexity of the organization's information technology infrastructure. A key component of the enterprise architecture is the embedded information security architecture that provides a roadmap to ensure that mission/business process-driven information security requirements and protection needs are defined and allocated to appropriate organizational information systems and the environments in which those systems operate.

2.4.1 Risk-Aware Mission/Business Processes

The risk management activities at Tier 2 begin with the identification and establishment of *risk-aware mission/business processes* to support the organizational missions and business functions. A risk-aware mission/business process is one that explicitly takes into account the likely risk such a process would cause if implemented. Risk aware processes are designed to manage risk in accordance with the risk management strategy defined at Tier 1 and explicitly account for risk when evaluating the mission/business activities and decisions at Tier 2.[34] Implementing risk-aware mission/business processes requires a thorough understanding of the organizational missions and business functions and the relationships among missions/business functions and supporting processes. This understanding is a prerequisite to building mission/business processes sufficiently resilient to withstand a wide variety of threats including routine and sophisticated cyber attacks, errors/accidents, and natural disasters. An important part of achieving risk-aware processes is the understanding of senior leaders/executives of: (i) the types of threat sources and threat events that can adversely affect the ability of organizations to successfully execute their missions/business functions); (ii) the potential adverse impacts/consequences on organizational operations and assets, individuals, other organizations, or the Nation if the confidentiality, integrity, or availability of information or information systems used in a mission/business process is compromised; and (iii) the likely resilience to such a compromise that can be achieved with a given mission/business process definition, applying realistic expectations for the resilience of information technology.

A key output from the Tier 2 definition of mission/business processes is the selected risk response strategy[35] for these processes within the constraints defined in the risk management strategy. The risk response strategy includes identification of information protection needs and the allocation of those needs across components of the process (e.g., allocation to protections within information systems, protections in the operational environments of those systems, and allocation to alternate mission/business execution paths based on the potential for compromise).

2.4.2 Enterprise Architecture

A significant risk-related issue regarding the ability of organizations to successfully carry out missions and business functions is the complexity of the information technology being used in information systems. To address this complexity and associated potential risk, organizations need a disciplined and structured approach for managing information technology assets supporting

---

[34] The identification of organizational mission/business processes includes defining the types of information that the organization needs to successfully execute those processes, the criticality and/or sensitivity of the information, and the information flows both internal and external to the organization.

[35] Risk response strategies are described in Appendix H.

their mission/business processes. Providing greater clarity and understanding of the information technology infrastructure of organizations including the design and development of the associated information systems is a prerequisite for maximizing the resilience and wise use of these systems in the face of increasingly sophisticated threats. This type of clarity and understanding can be effectively achieved through the development and implementation of enterprise architecture.

Enterprise architecture is a management practice employed by organizations to maximize the effectiveness of mission/business processes and information resources in helping to achieve mission/business success. Enterprise architecture establishes a clear and unambiguous connection from investments (including information security investments) to measurable performance improvements whether for an entire organization or portion of an organization. Enterprise architecture also provides an opportunity to standardize, consolidate, and optimize information technology assets. These activities ultimately produce information systems that are more transparent and therefore, easier to understand and protect. In addition to establishing a roadmap for more efficient and cost-effective usage of information technology throughout organizations, enterprise architecture provides a common language for discussing risk management issues related to missions, business processes, and performance goals—enabling better coordination and integration of efforts and investments across organizational and business activity boundaries. A well-designed enterprise architecture implemented organization-wide, promotes more efficient, cost-effective, consistent, and interoperable information security capabilities to help organizations better protect missions and business functions—and ultimately more effectively manage risk.

The Federal Enterprise Architecture (FEA) defines a collection of interrelated *reference models* including Performance, Business, Service Component, Data, and Technical as well as more detailed *segment* and *solution* architectures that are derived from the *enterprise* architecture.[36] Organizational assets (including programs, processes, information, applications, technology, investments, personnel, and facilities) are mapped to the enterprise-level reference models to create a segment-oriented view of organizations. Segments are elements of organizations describing mission areas, common/shared business services, and organization-wide services. From an investment perspective, segment architecture drives decisions for a business case or group of business cases supporting specific mission areas or common/shared services. The primary stakeholders for segment architecture are mission/business owners. Following closely from segment architecture, solution architecture defines the information technology assets within organizations used to automate and improve mission/business processes. The scope of solution architecture is typically used to develop and implement all or parts of information systems or business solutions, including information security solutions. The primary stakeholders for solution architectures are information system developers and integrators, information system owners, information system/security engineers, and end users.

> *The FEA concepts that define needs-driven, performance-based business processes are applied by organizations, recognizing that effectively managing risk arising from operating in a cyberspace environment with sophisticated, high-end threats is a key need and measure of performance.*

---

[36] The Federal Enterprise Architecture is described in a series of documents published by the OMB FEA Program Management Office. Additional information on the FEA reference models and the segment and solution architectures can be found in the FEA Consolidated Reference Model Document and FEA Practice Guidance, respectively.

Enterprise architecture also promotes the concepts of *segmentation, redundancy*, and elimination of *single points of failure*—all concepts that can help organizations more effectively manage risk. Segmentation is important because it allows organizations to separate missions/business functions and operations and the information systems, system components, or subsystems supporting those missions, functions, and operations from other functions and operations and supporting systems. Segmentation helps to define more manageable components and to potentially reduce the degree of harm from a successful threat exploitation of a vulnerability. Segment architecture supports the concept of segmentation at the highest levels of organizations and the concept is carried forward through solution architecture (including decomposition of information systems and networks into subsystems and subnetworks, as appropriate).

The concept of redundancy is also very important in enterprise architecture. With the high probability of breaches or compromises when threats exploit vulnerabilities in organizational information systems, the failure or degradation of one or more information system components is inevitable. To enhance information system resilience as part of risk response, organizational information systems provide a failover mode that helps to ensure that failed components trigger appropriate backup components with similar capability. This type of capability is essential to address the advanced persistent threat in situations where organizations might be required to operate while under cyber attack in a degraded mode but still providing a sufficient level of capability to achieve mission/business success. Segment and solution architectures support the concept of redundancy by establishing a disciplined and structured approach to developing and implementing key architectural considerations that facilitate replication of critical information system components, where appropriate.

Finally, the concept of single point of failure and the elimination of such failure points is easily supported by enterprise architecture. Having the essential visibility and transparency provided in the architectural design at the organization level exposes potential single points of failure early in the development process. Thus, single points of failure are effectively addressed by segment and solution architectures. Failure to address potential single points of failure early in the architectural design can result in severe or catastrophic effects when those failure points are propagated to information systems and the actual failure causes a loss of mission/business capability.

2.4.3 Information Security Architecture

The *information security architecture* is an integral part of the organization's enterprise architecture. It represents that portion of the enterprise architecture specifically addressing information system resilience and providing architectural information for the implementation of security capabilities.[37] The primary purpose of the information security architecture is to ensure that mission/business process-driven *information security requirements* are consistently and cost-effectively achieved in organizational information systems and the environments in which those systems operate consistent with the organizational risk management strategy.[38] The information security architecture also incorporates security requirements from legislation, directives, policies, regulations, standards, and guidance into the segment architecture. Ultimately, the information security architecture provides a detailed roadmap that allows traceability from the highest-level strategic goals and objectives of organizations, through specific mission/business protection needs, to specific information security solutions provided by people, processes, and technologies.

---

[37] In general, a version of an information security architecture exists for each of the enterprise architecture *reference models;* including Performance, Business, Service Component, Data, and Technical.

[38] Organizations employ sound system and security engineering principles and techniques to ensure that information security requirements are effectively implemented in organizational information systems.

Information security requirements defined in the segment architecture are implemented in the solution architecture in the form of management, operational, and technical *security controls*. The security controls are employed within or inherited by the individual information systems and the environments in which the systems operate. The allocation[39] of security controls is consistent with the information security architecture as well as concepts such as *defense-in-depth* and *defense-in-breadth*. Figure 3 illustrates the process of integrating information security requirements into the enterprise architecture and the associated information systems supporting the mission/business processes of organizations.

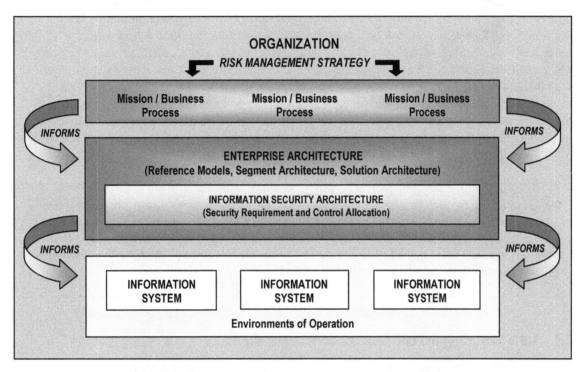

FIGURE 3: INFORMATION SECURITY REQUIREMENTS INTEGRATION

To summarize, risk management considerations can be addressed as an integral part of the enterprise architecture by:

- Developing a segment architecture linked to the strategic goals and objectives of organizations, defined missions/business functions, and associated mission/business processes;

- Identifying where effective risk response is a critical element in the success of organizational missions and business functions;

- Defining the appropriate, architectural-level information security requirements within organization-defined segments based on the organization's risk management strategy;

- Incorporating an information security architecture that implements architectural-level information security requirements;

---

[39] Security control allocation occurs down to the information system component level, employing security controls in selected system components assigned to provide a specific security capability. Specific guidance on how to incorporate information security requirements into enterprise architecture is provided in the FEA Security and Privacy Profile.

- Translating the information security requirements from the segment architecture into specific security controls for information systems/environments of operation as part of the solution architecture;

- Allocating management, operational, and technical security controls to information systems and environments of operation as defined by the information security architecture; and

- Documenting risk management decisions at all levels of the enterprise architecture.[40]

Enterprise architecture provides a disciplined and structured approach to achieving consolidation, standardization, and optimization of information technology assets that are employed within organizations. Risk reduction can be achieved through the full integration of management processes[41] organization-wide, thereby providing greater degrees of security, privacy, reliability, and cost-effectiveness for the missions and business functions being carried out by organizations. This integrated approach of incorporating the organization's risk management strategy into enterprise architecture gives senior leaders/executives the opportunity to make more informed risk-based decisions in dynamic operating environments—decisions based on trade-offs between fulfilling and improving organizational missions and business functions and managing the many types and sources of risk that must be considered in their risk management responsibilities.

> *The use of enterprise architecture can greatly enhance an organization's risk posture by providing greater transparency and clarity in design and development activities—enabling a more consistent application of the principle of 'wise use' of technologies across the organization; optimizing the trade-offs between value gained from and the risk being incurred through the information systems supporting organizational missions/business functions.*

2.5 TIER THREE—INFORMATION SYSTEMS VIEW

All information systems, including operational systems, systems under development, and systems undergoing modification, are in some phase of the system development life cycle.[42] In addition to the risk management activities carried out at Tier 1 and Tier 2 (e.g., reflecting the organization's risk management strategy within the enterprise architecture and embedded information security architecture), risk management activities are also integrated into the system development life cycle of organizational information systems at Tier 3. The risk management activities at Tier 3 reflect the organization's risk management strategy and any risk related to the cost, schedule, and performance requirements for individual information systems supporting the mission/business functions of organizations. Risk management activities take place at every phase in the system development life cycle with the outputs at each phase having an effect on subsequent phases.

---

[40] The activities required to effectively incorporate information security into enterprise architecture are carried out by key stakeholders within organizations including mission/business owners, chief information officers, chief information security officers, authorizing officials, and the risk executive (function).

[41] A management process is a process for planning and controlling the performance or execution of organizational activities (e.g., programs, projects, tasks, processes). Management processes are often referred to as performance measurement and management systems.

[42] There are typically five phases in system development life cycles: (i) *initiation*; (ii) *development/ acquisition*; (iii) *implementation*; (iv) *operation/maintenance*; and (v) *disposal*. Organizations may use a variety of system development life cycle processes including, for example, waterfall, spiral, or agile development.

For example, requirements definition[43] is a critical part of any system development process and begins very early in the life cycle, typically in the *initiation* phase. The latest threat information that is available to organizations, or current organizational assumptions concerning threat, may significantly influence information system requirements and the types of solutions that are deemed by organizations to be acceptable (from a technological and operational perspective) in the face of such threats. Information security requirements are a subset of the functional requirements levied on information systems and are incorporated into the system development life cycle simultaneously with the other requirements. The information security requirements define the needed security functionality[44] for information systems and the level of trustworthiness for that functionality (see Section 2.6 on the trustworthiness of information systems).

Organizations also address risk management issues during the *development/acquisition* phase of the system development life cycle (e.g., system design, system development/integration, and demonstration). Whether in response to specific and credible threat information or assumptions about the threat, potential design-related vulnerabilities in organizational information systems can be mitigated during this phase by choosing less susceptible alternatives. Supply chain risk during the acquisition phase of the information system is also an area of concern for organizations. To address supply chain risk during the development/acquisition phase, organizations implement specific security controls as deemed necessary by the organization. Organizations also consider risk from the standpoint of the environment in which the information systems are intended to operate when selecting the most appropriate security controls. To be effective, controls must be mutually supporting, employed with realistic expectations for effectiveness, and implemented as part of an explicit, information system-level security architecture that is consistent with the security architecture embedded in the organization's enterprise architecture. For example, when certain technical controls are less than effective due to achievable levels of trustworthiness in organizational information systems, management and operational controls are employed as compensating controls—thus providing another opportunity to manage risk.

Subsequent to initiation, development, and acquisition, the *implementation* phase of the system development life cycle provides an opportunity for the organization to determine the effectiveness of the selected security controls employed within or inherited by the information systems under development prior to the commencement of actual operations. Expectations generated during this phase can be compared with actual behavior as information systems are implemented. Given the current threat information that is available to organizations and organizational assumptions about the threat, the information discovered during effectiveness assessments, and the potential adverse impacts on organizational missions/business functions, it may be necessary to modify or change the planned implementation of the information system. Risk-related information can be developed to justify the proposed changes.

Once approved for operation, information systems move into the *operations/maintenance* phase of the system development life cycle. The monitoring of security control effectiveness and any changes to organizational information systems and the environments in which those systems operate ensure that selected risk response measures are operating as intended on an ongoing basis. Ongoing monitoring is paramount to maintaining situational awareness of risk to organizational missions and business functions—an awareness that is critical to making the necessary course

---

[43] Information security requirements can be obtained from a variety of sources (e.g., legislation, policies, directives, regulations, standards, and organizational mission/business/operational requirements).

[44] Security functionality is the set of security controls employed within or inherited by an information system or the environment in which the system operates. The security controls, described in NIST Special Publication 800-53, are implemented by a combination of people, processes, and technologies.

corrections when risk exceeds organizational risk tolerance. During the *disposal* phase of the system development life cycle, it is standard procedure for organizations to verifiably remove prior to disposal, any information from information systems that may cause adverse impacts, if compromised, and also assess any risk associated with these activities.[45]

Early integration of information security requirements into the system development life cycle is the most cost-effective method for implementing the organizational risk management strategy at Tier 3.[46] Incorporating risk management into the system development life cycle ensures that the risk management process is not isolated from the other management processes employed by the organization to develop, acquire, implement, operate, and maintain the information systems supporting organizational missions and business functions. To support system development life cycle integration, risk management (including information security considerations) is also incorporated into program, planning, and budgeting activities to help ensure that appropriate resources are available when needed—thus facilitating the completion of program and project milestones established by organizations. To incorporate risk management into program, planning and budgeting activities, risk and information security professionals are an integral part of the teams and structures used to address information system and organizational requirements.

The overall *resilience* of organizational information systems (i.e., how well systems operate while under stress) is a key factor and performance measure in determining the potential survivability of missions/business functions. The use of certain information technologies may introduce inherent vulnerabilities into these information systems—resulting in risk that may have to be mitigated by reengineering the current mission/business processes. The *wise use* of information technologies during the design, development, and implementation of organizational information systems is of paramount importance in managing risk.

> *Making information security-related requirements and activities an integral part of the system development life cycle ensures that senior leaders/executives consider the risks to organizational operations and assets, individuals, other organizations, and the Nation resulting from the operation and use of information systems and take appropriate actions to exercise the organization's due diligence.*

2.6 TRUST AND TRUSTWORTHINESS

Trust is an important concept related to risk management. How organizations approach trust influences their behaviors and their internal and external trust relationships. This section introduces some conceptual ways of thinking about trust, defines the concept of *trustworthiness*, and shows how the concept of trustworthiness can be used in developing *trust relationships*. Appendix G describes several *trust models* that can be applied in an organizational context, and

---

[45] While the presentation of the system development life cycle is expressed as a linear flow, in reality, the knowledge gained during a later phase of the life cycle or changes in system requirements or operational environments may dictate revisiting an earlier phase. For example, changes in the threat environment during the operation/maintenance phrase may dictate the need to initiate a new or revised system capability.

[46] The Risk Management Framework (RMF), described in NIST Special Publication 800-37, provides a structured process that integrates risk management activities into the system development life cycle. The RMF operates primarily at Tier 3 but also interacts with Tier 1 and Tier 2 (e.g., providing feedback from authorization decisions to the risk executive [function], disseminating updated risk information to authorizing officials, common control providers, and information system owners).

considers how trust can be measured. The importance of organizational governance, culture, and transparency[47] are also considered with regard to trust and its affect on risk management.

Trust is a belief that an entity will behave in a predictable manner in specified circumstances. The entity may be a person, process, object or any combination of such components. The entity can be of any size from a single hardware component or software module, to a piece of equipment identified by make and model, to a site or location, to an organization, to a nation-state. Trust, while inherently a subjective determination, can be based on objective evidence and subjective elements. The objective grounds for trust can include for example, the results of information technology product testing and evaluation. Subjective belief, level of comfort, and experience may supplement (or even replace) objective evidence, or substitute for such evidence when it is unavailable. Trust is usually relative to a specific circumstance or situation (e.g., the amount of money involved in a transaction, the sensitivity or criticality of information, or whether safety is an issue with human lives at stake). Trust is generally not transitive (e.g., you trust a friend but not necessarily a friend of a friend). Finally, trust is generally earned, based on experience or measurement. However, in certain organizations, trust may be mandated by policy (see Appendix G, *mandated trust model*).

Trustworthiness is an attribute of a person or organization that provides confidence to others of the qualifications, capabilities, and reliability of that entity to perform specific tasks and fulfill assigned responsibilities. Trustworthiness is also a characteristic of information technology products and systems (see Section 2.6.2 on *trustworthiness of information systems*). The attribute of trustworthiness, whether applied to people, processes, or technologies, can be measured, at least in relative terms if not quantitatively.[48] The determination of trustworthiness plays a key role in establishing trust relationships among persons and organizations. The trust relationships are key factors in risk decisions made by senior leaders/executives.

2.6.1 Establishing Trust Among Organizations

Parties enter into trust relationships based on mission and business needs.[49] Trust among parties typically exists along a continuum with varying degrees of trust achieved based on a number of factors. Organizations can still share information and obtain information technology services even if their trust relationship falls short of complete trust. The degree of trust required for organizations to establish partnerships can vary widely based on many factors including the organizations involved and the specifics of the situation (e.g., the missions, goals, and objectives of the potential partners, the criticality/sensitivity of activities involved in the partnership, the risk tolerance of the organizations participating in the partnership, and the historical relationship among the participants). Finally, the degree of trust among entities is not a static quality but can vary over time as circumstances change.

---

[47] *Transparency* is achieved by providing *visibility* into the risk management and information security activities carried out by organizations participating in partnerships (e.g., employing common security standards, specification language for security controls including common controls, assessment procedures, risk assessment methodologies; defining common artifacts and bodies of evidence used in making risk-related decisions).

[48] Current state-of-the-practice for measuring *trustworthiness* can reliably differentiate between widely different levels of trustworthiness and is capable of producing a trustworthiness scale that is hierarchical between similar instances of measuring activities (e.g., the results from ISO/IEC 15408 [Common Criteria] evaluations).

[49] Trust relationships can be: (i) formally established, for example, by documenting the trust-related information in contracts, service-level agreements, statements of work, memoranda of agreement/understanding, or interconnection security agreements; (ii) scalable and inter-organizational or intra-organizational in nature; and/or (iii) represented by simple (bilateral) relationships between two partners or more complex many-to many relationships among many diverse partners.

Organizations are becoming increasingly reliant on information system services[50] and information provided by external organizations as well as partnerships to accomplish missions and business functions. This reliance results in the need for *trust relationships* among organizations.[51] In many cases, trust relationships with external organizations, while generating greater productivity and cost efficiencies, can also bring greater risk to organizations. This risk is addressed by the risk management strategies established by organizations that take into account the strategic goals and objectives of organizations.

Effectively addressing the risk associated with the growing dependence on external service providers and partnerships with domestic and international public and private sector participants necessitates that organizations:

- Define the types of services/information to be provided to organizations or the types of information to be shared/exchanged in any proposed partnering arrangements;

- Establish the degree of control or influence organizations have over the external organizations participating in such partnering arrangements;

- Describe how the services/information are to be protected in accordance with the information security requirements of organizations;

- Obtain the relevant information from external organizations to determine trustworthiness and to support and maintain trust (e.g., visibility into business practices and risk/information security decisions to understand risk tolerance);

- Appropriately balance mission/business-based requirements to support information sharing while considering the risk of working with competing or hostile entities and the risk that other organizations, while neither competing or hostile, may be a path through which such entities attack;

- Determine if the ongoing risk to organizational operations and assets, individuals, other organizations, or the Nation resulting from the continuing use of the services/information or the participation in the partnership, is at an acceptable level; and

- Recognize that decisions to establish trust relationships are expressions of acceptable risk.

The degree of trust that an organization places in external organizations can vary widely, ranging from those who are highly trusted (e.g., business partners in a joint venture that share a common business model and common goals) to those who are less trusted and may represent greater sources of risk (e.g., business partners in one endeavor who are also competitors or adversaries). The specifics of establishing and maintaining trust can differ from organization to organization based on mission/business requirements, the participants involved in the trust relationship, the criticality/sensitivity of the information being shared or the types of services being rendered, the history between the organizations, and the overall risk to the organizations participating in the relationship. Appendix G provides several trust models that organizations can use when dealing with external organizations.

In many situations, the trust established between organizations may not allow a full spectrum of information sharing or a complete provision of services. When an organization determines that

---

[50] External information system services are services that are implemented outside of the system's traditional authorization boundary (i.e., services that are used by, but not a part of, the organizational information system).

[51] External providers or mission/business partners can be public or private sector entities, domestic or international.

the trustworthiness of another organization does not permit the complete sharing of information or use of external services, the organization can: (i) mitigate risk, transfer risk, or share risk by employing one or more compensating controls; (ii) accept a greater degree of risk; or (iii) avoid risk by performing missions/business functions with reduced levels of functionality or possibly no functionality at all.

Explicit understanding and acceptance of the risk to an organization's operations and assets, individuals, other organizations, and the Nation by senior leaders/executives (reflecting the organization's risk tolerance) are made in accordance with the organization's risk management strategy and a prerequisite for establishing trust relationships among organizations.

2.6.2 Trustworthiness of Information Systems

The concept of trustworthiness can also be applied to information systems and the information technology products and services that compose those systems. Trustworthiness expresses the degree to which information systems (including the information technology products from which the systems are built) can be expected to preserve the confidentiality, integrity, and availability of the information being processed, stored, or transmitted by the systems across the full range of threats. Trustworthy information systems are systems that have been determined to have the level of trustworthiness necessary to operate within defined levels of *risk* despite the environmental disruptions, human errors, and purposeful attacks that are expected to occur in their environments of operation. Two factors affecting the trustworthiness of information systems are:

- *Security functionality* (i.e., the security features/functions employed within the system); and

- *Security assurance* (i.e., the grounds for confidence that the security functionality is effective in its application).[52]

Security functionality can be obtained by employing within organizational information systems and their environments of operation, a combination of management, operational, and technical security controls from NIST Special Publication 800-53.[53] The development and implementation of needed security controls is guided by and informed by the enterprise architecture established by organizations.

Security assurance is a critical aspect in determining the trustworthiness of information systems. Assurance is the measure of confidence that the security features, practices, procedures, and architecture of an information system accurately mediates and enforces the security policy.[54] Assurance is obtained by: (i) the actions taken by developers and implementers[55] with regard to the design, development, implementation, and operation of the security functionality (i.e., security controls); and (ii) the actions taken by assessors to determine the extent to which the functionality is implemented correctly, operating as intended, and producing the desired outcome

---

[52] Assurance also represents the grounds for confidence that the intended functionality of an information system is correct, always invoked (when needed), and resistant to bypass or tampering.

[53] The employment of appropriate security controls for information systems and environments of operation is guided by the first three steps in the Risk Management Framework (i.e., categorization, selection, and implementation).

[54] A *security policy* is set of criteria for the provision of security services.

[55] In this context, a developer/implementer is an individual or group of individuals responsible for the design, development, implementation, or operation of security controls for an information system or supporting infrastructure.

with respect to meeting the security requirements for information systems and their environments of operation.[56] Developers and implementers can increase the assurance in security functionality by employing well-defined security policies and policy models, structured and rigorous hardware and software development techniques, and sound system/security engineering principles.

Assurance for information technology products and systems is commonly based on the assessments conducted (and associated assessment evidence produced) during the initiation, acquisition/development, implementation, and operations/maintenance phases of the system development life cycle. For example, developmental evidence may include the techniques and methods used to design and develop security functionality. Operational evidence may include flaw reporting and remediation, the results of security incident reporting, and the results of ongoing security control monitoring. Independent assessments by qualified assessors may include analyses of the evidence as well as testing, inspections, and audits of the implementation of the selected security functionality.[57]

The concepts of assurance and trustworthiness are closely related. Assurance contributes to the trustworthiness determination relative to an information technology product or an information system. Developers/implementers of information technology products or systems may provide assurance evidence by generating appropriate artifacts (e.g., the results of independent testing and evaluation, design documentation, high-level or low-level specifications, source code analysis). Organizations using information technology products or systems may perform, or rely on others to perform, some form of assessment on the products or systems. Organizations may also have direct experience with the product or system, or may receive information about the performance of the product or system from third parties. Organizations typically evaluate all of the available assurance evidence, often applying different weighting factors as appropriate, to determine the trustworthiness of the product or system relative to the circumstances.

Information technology products and systems exhibiting a higher degree of trustworthiness (i.e., products/systems having appropriate functionality and assurance) are expected to exhibit a lower rate of latent design and implementation flaws and a higher degree of penetration resistance against a range of threats including sophisticated cyber attacks, natural disasters, accidents, and intentional/unintentional errors. The susceptibility of missions/business functions of organizations to known threats, the environments of operation where information systems are deployed, and the maximum acceptable level of risk to organizational operations and assets, individuals, other organizations, or the Nation, guide the degree of trustworthiness needed.

Trustworthiness is a key factor in the selection and wise use of information technology products used in organizational information systems. Insufficient attention to trustworthiness of information technology products and systems can adversely affect an organization's capability to successfully carry out its assigned missions/business functions.

---

[56] For other than national security systems, organizations meet minimum assurance requirements specified in NIST Special Publication 800-53, Appendix E.

[57] NIST Special Publication 800-53A provides guidance on assessing security controls in federal information systems.

2.7 ORGANIZATIONAL CULTURE

Organizational *culture* refers to the values, beliefs, and norms that influence the behaviors and actions of the senior leaders/executives and individual members of organizations. Culture describes the way things are done in organizations and can explain why certain things occur. There is a direct relationship between organizational culture and how organizations respond to uncertainties and the potential for near-term benefits to be the source for longer-term losses. The organization's culture informs and even, to perhaps a large degree, defines that organization's risk management strategy. At a minimum, when an expressed risk management strategy is not consistent with that organization's culture, then it is likely that the strategy will be difficult if not impossible to implement. Recognizing and addressing the significant influence culture has on risk-related decisions of senior leaders/executives within organizations can therefore, be key to achieving effective management of risk.

Recognizing the impact from organizational culture on the implementation of an organization-wide risk management program is important as this can reflect a major organizational change. This change must be effectively managed and understanding the culture of an organization plays an important part in achieving such organization-wide change. Implementing an effective risk management program may well represent a significant organization-wide change aligning the people, processes, and culture within the organization with the new or revised organizational goals and objectives, the risk management strategy, and communication mechanisms for sharing risk-related information among entities. To effectively manage such change, organizations include cultural considerations as a fundamental component in their strategic-level thinking and decision-making processes (e.g., developing the risk management strategy). If the senior leaders/executives understand the importance of culture, they have a better chance of achieving the organization's strategic goals and objectives by successfully managing risk.

Culture also impacts the degree of risk being incurred. Culture is reflected in an organization's willingness to adopt new and leading edge information technologies. For example, organizations that are engaged in research and development activities may be more likely to push technological boundaries. Such organizations are more prone to be early adopters of new technologies and therefore, more likely to view the new technologies from the standpoint of the potential benefits achieved versus potential harm from use. In contrast, organizations that are engaged in security-related activities may be more conservative by nature and less likely to push technological boundaries—being more suspicious of the new technologies, especially if provided by some entity with which the organization lacks familiarity and trust. These types of organizations are also less likely to be early adopters of new technologies and would be more inclined to look at the potential harm caused by the adoption of the new technologies. Another example is that some organizations have a history of developing proprietary software applications and services, or procuring software applications and services solely for their use. These organizations may be reluctant to use externally-provided software applications and services and this reluctance may result in lower risk being incurred. Other organizations may, on the other hand, seek to maximize advantages achieved by modern net-centric architectures (e.g., service-oriented architectures, cloud computing), where hardware, software, and services are typically provided by external organizations. Since organizations typically do not have direct control over assessment, auditing, and oversight activities of external providers, a greater risk might be incurred.

In addition to the cultural impacts on organizational risk management perspectives, there can also be cultural issues between organizations. Where two or more organizations are operating together toward a common purpose, there is a possibility that cultural differences in each of the respective organizations may result in different risk management strategies, propensity to incur risk, and willingness to accept risk.[58] For example, assume two organizations are working together to create a common security service intended to address the advanced persistent threat. The culture of one of the organizations may result in a focus on preventing unauthorized disclosure of information, while the nature of the other organization may result in an emphasis on mission continuity. The differences in focus and emphasis resulting from organizational culture can generate different priorities and expectations regarding what security services to procure, because the organizations perceive the nature of the threat differently. Such culture-related disconnects do not occur solely between organizations but can also occur within organizations, where different organizational components (e.g., information technology components, operational components) have different values and perhaps risk tolerances. An example of an internal disconnect can be observed in a hospital that emphasizes different cultures between protecting the personal privacy of patients and the availability of medical information to medical professionals for treatment purposes.

Culture both shapes and is shaped by the people within organizations. Cultural influences and impacts can be felt across all three tiers in the multitiered risk management approach. Senior leaders/executives both directly and indirectly in Tier 1 governance structures set the stage for how organizations respond to various approaches to managing risk. Senior leaders/executives establish the risk tolerance for organizations both formally (e.g., through publication of strategy and guidance documents) and informally (e.g., through actions that get rewarded and penalized, the degree of consistency in actions, and the degree of accountability enforced). The direction set by senior leaders/executives and the understanding of existing organizational values and priorities are major factors determining how risk is managed within organizations.

2.8 RELATIONSHIP AMONG KEY RISK CONCEPTS

As indicated by the discussions above, there are a variety of risk-related concepts (e.g., risk tolerance, trust, and culture), all of which have an impact on risk management. The concepts do not operate in a vacuum; rather, there is often a strong interplay among the concepts (e.g., an organization's culture along with its governance structures and processes, often influences the pace of change and the implementation of its risk management strategy). For this reason, the risk executive (function) and other parties involved in organizational risk-based decisions, need to have an awareness and appreciation for all of the concepts. Several examples of the relationships among the risk-related concepts are provided below. The list of relationships is not exhaustive and serves only to illustrate how combining risk-related concepts can produce unintended consequences, both positive and negative in scope.

2.8.1 Governance, Risk Tolerance, and Trust

As part of implementing the organization's risk management strategy at Tier 1, the risk executive (function) establishes practices for sharing risk-related information with external entities. With regard to the demonstration of due diligence for managing risk, organizations that are less risk tolerant are likely to require more supporting evidence than organizations that are more risk tolerant. Such organizations may only trust (and hence partner with) organizations with which they have had a long and successful relationship (see direct historical trust model in Appendix G). The amount of centralization[59] within an organization may be reflective of the organizational risk tolerance and/or its willingness to trust partnering organizations. Some organizations select a

---

[58] A similar situation can exist between subordinate elements of an organization when these elements are afforded a fair amount of autonomy and operational authority.

[59] Additional information on governance models can be found in Appendix F.

decentralized governance structure for reasons such as widely diverging mission/business areas or need for increased separation between mission/business lines due to sensitivity of the work. The reasons for decentralization may reflect and likely will influence risk tolerance. For instance, if there are no partnering organizations meeting the established trust qualifications, less risk-tolerant organizations may require significantly more supporting evidence of due diligence (e.g., access to risk assessments, security plans, security assessment reports, risk acceptance decisions) than is typically required in such situations (see validated trust model in Appendix G).

2.8.2 Trust and Culture

There is also potential interplay between the concepts of risk, trust, and culture. Changes in mission/business requirements (e.g., a new mission or business requirement to interconnect information systems for the purpose of sharing information) may require a greater acceptance of risk than is typical for that organization. In the short term, additional measures may be needed to establish and/or build trust (e.g., increase transparency between interconnecting organizations). Such measures facilitate building trust and evolving organizational beliefs and norms over the longer term. Interaction between trust and culture can also be observed when there are gaps and overlaps in responsibility among an organization's components that may impact the ability for proposed actions (especially new actions) to be carried out quickly. For example, many organizations with decentralized governance structures may be slower to embrace change unless there has been an extensive effort to expand coordination and improve trust among organizational components. Assume that some organizations are directed by higher authorities (see mandated trust model in Appendix G) to share information more freely with peer organizations. If the organizations have a history and culture of tightly controlling information, they may be reluctance to share information with outside entities, even though directed to do so. In such situations, organizations may require that partnering organizations provide concrete evidence of the steps taken to protect the information designated for sharing prior to release.

2.8.3 Investment Strategy and Risk Tolerance

Investment strategies and organizational risk tolerance also have linkages. Organizations may recognize that there is a need to address advanced persistent threats where adversaries have achieved some degree of penetration of and foothold within organizational information systems and the environments in which those systems operate. The strategic investments that are required to address these types of threats may, in part, be influenced by the risk tolerance of organizations. Less risk-tolerant organizations may focus investments on information technologies that prevent adversaries from gaining further access within organizations and/or limiting the damage done to the organizations even if at the expense of achieving some of the many mission/business benefits automation can provide. More risk-tolerant organizations may focus investments on information technologies that provide greater mission/business benefits even if these benefits are achieved at the expense of adversaries gaining some advantage or benefit from compromising the information systems and supporting infrastructure.

2.8.4 Culture and Risk Tolerance

A major part of managing risk within organizations is identifying what the organizational risk tolerance is for a particular type of loss. Risk tolerance can be described as a combination of the cultural willingness to accept certain types of loss within organizations and the subjective risk-related actions of senior leaders/executives. Risk-based decisions within organizations often reflect the blending of the risk tolerance of senior leaders/executives and the risk tolerance that is embedded within the culture of organizations. In establishing organizational risk tolerance, the values, beliefs, and norms of organizations are examined in order to understand why risk trade-offs are made. For some organizations, in particular those organizations that deal with critical and/or sensitive information, personally identifiable information, or classified information, the emphasis is often on preventing unauthorized disclosure. In contrast, in those organizations driven by a combination of organizational culture and the nature of their missions and business functions, the emphasis is on maintaining the availability of information systems to achieve an ongoing operational capability. As part of establishing organizational risk tolerance, a risk assessment identifies the kinds and levels of risk to which organizations may be exposed. This assessment considers both the likelihood and impact of undesired events (see Chapter Three, the risk management process).

CHAPTER THREE

THE PROCESS

APPLYING RISK MANAGEMENT CONCEPTS ACROSS AN ORGANIZATION

This chapter describes a process for managing information security risk including: (i) a general overview of the risk management process; (ii) how organizations establish the context for risk-based decisions; (iii) how organizations assess risk considering threats, vulnerabilities, likelihood, and consequences/impact; (iv) how organizations respond to risk once determined; and (v) how organizations monitor risk over time with changing mission/business needs, operating environments, and supporting information systems . The risk management process, introduced in Chapter Two, is described in this chapter along with its applicability across the three tiers of risk management. Each of the steps in the risk management process (i.e., risk framing, risk assessment, risk response, and risk monitoring) is described in a structured manner focusing on the *inputs* or *preconditions* necessary to initiate the step, the specific *activities* that compose the step, and the *outputs* or *post conditions* resulting from the step.[60] The effect of the risk concepts described in Chapter Two (e.g., risk tolerance, trust, and culture) are also discussed in the context of the risk management process and its multitiered application. Figure 4 illustrates the risk management process as applied across the tiers—organization, mission/business process, and information system. The bidirectional arrows in the figure indicate that the information and communication flows among the risk management components as well as the execution order of the components, may be flexible and respond to the dynamic nature of the risk management process as it is applied across all three tiers.

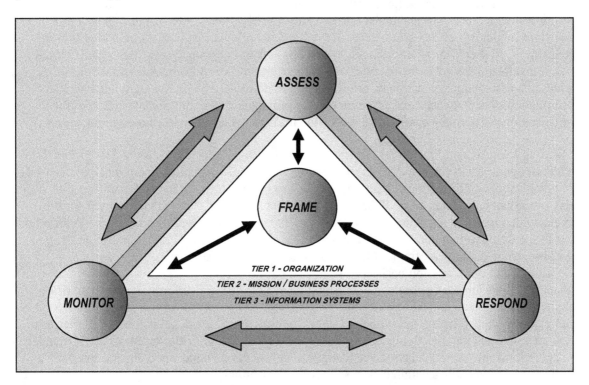

FIGURE 4: RISK MANAGEMENT PROCESS APPLIED ACROSS THE TIERS

---

[60] Additional guidance on selected steps in the risk management process (e.g., risk assessment, risk monitoring) can be found in other NIST Special Publications listed in Appendix A.

The steps in the risk management process are not inherently sequential in nature. The steps are performed in different ways, depending on the particular tier where the step is applied and on prior activities related to each of the steps. What is consistent is that the outputs or post conditions from a particular risk management step directly impact one or more of the other risk management steps in the risk management process. Organizations have significant flexibility in how the risk management steps are performed (e.g., sequence, degree of rigor, formality, and thoroughness of application) and in how the results of each step are captured and shared—both internally and externally. Ultimately, the objective of applying the risk management process and associated risk-related concepts is to develop a better understanding of information security risk in the context of the broader actions and decisions of organizations and in particular, with respect to organizational operations and assets, individuals, other organizations, and Nation.

3.1 FRAMING RISK

Risk framing establishes the context and provides a common perspective on how organizations manage risk. Risk framing, as its principal output, produces a *risk management strategy* that addresses how organizations intend to assess risk, respond to risk, and monitor risk. The risk management strategy makes explicit the specific assumptions, constraints, risk tolerances, and priorities/trade-offs used within organizations for making investment and operational decisions. The risk management strategy also includes any strategic-level decisions and considerations on how risk to organizational operations and assets, individuals, other organizations, and the Nation, is to be managed by senior leaders/executives.

At Tier 1, senior leaders/executives, in consultation and collaboration with the risk executive (function), define the organizational risk frame including the types of risk decisions (e.g., risk responses) supported, how and under what conditions risk is assessed to support those risk decisions, and how risk is monitored (e.g., to what level of detail, in what form, and with what frequency). At Tier 2, mission/business owners apply their understanding of the organizational risk frame to address concerns specific to the organization's missions/business functions (e.g., additional assumptions, constraints, priorities, and trade-offs). At Tier 3, program managers, information system owners, and common control providers apply their understanding of the organizational risk frame based on how decision makers at Tiers 1 and 2 choose to manage risk.

The Risk Management Framework[61] is the primary means for addressing risk at Tier 3. The RMF addresses concerns specific to the design, development, implementation, operation, and disposal of organizational information systems and the environments in which those systems operate. The risk frame can be adapted at Tier 3 based on the current phase of the system development life cycle, which further constrains potential risk responses. Initially, organizational risk frames might not be explicit or might not be defined in terms that correspond to the risk management tiers. In the absence of explicit risk frames (describing assumptions, constraints, risk tolerance, and priorities/trade-offs), mission/business owners can have divergent perspectives on risk or how to manage it. This impedes a common understanding at Tier 1 of how information security risk contributes to organizational risk, and at Tier 2, of how risk accepted for one mission or business function potentially affects risk with respect to other missions/business functions. Differences in risk tolerance and the underlying assumptions, constraints, and priorities/trade-offs are grounded in operational and/or architectural considerations and should be understood and accepted by senior leaders/executives within their respective organizations.

---

[61] The Risk Management Framework (RMF) which operates primarily at Tier 3 is described in NIST Special Publication 800-37.

STEP 1: RISK FRAMING

Inputs and Preconditions

Risk framing is the set of assumptions, constraints, risk tolerances, and priorities/trade-offs that shape an organization's approach for managing risk. Risk framing is informed by the organizational governance structure, financial posture, legal/regulatory environment, investment strategy, culture, and trust relationships established within and among organizations. Inputs to the risk framing step include, for example, laws, policies, directives, regulations, contractual relationships, and financial limitations which impose constraints on potential risk decisions by organizations. Other inputs to risk framing can include, for example, specific information from organizations to make explicit: (i) the identification of trust relationships and trust models (see Appendix G) that derive from existing memoranda of understanding or agreement (MOUs or MOAs); and (ii) the identification of the governance structures and processes that indicate the extent of or limits on decision-making authority for risk decisions that can be delegated to mission or business owners. The key precondition for risk framing is senior leadership commitment to defining an explicit risk management strategy and holding mission/business owners responsible and accountable for implementing the strategy.

The guidance produced by the risk framing step, and the underlying assumptions, constraints, risk tolerances, and priorities/trade-offs used to develop that guidance, may be inappropriate to one or more organizational missions or business functions. In addition, the risk environment has the potential to change over time. Thus, the risk management process allows for feedback to the risk framing step from the other steps in the process, as follows:

- *Risk assessment:* Information generated during the risk assessment may influence the original assumptions, change the constraints regarding appropriate risk responses, identify additional tradeoffs, or shift priorities. For example, the characterization of adversaries (including representative tactics, techniques, and procedures), or sources of vulnerability information may not be consistent with how some organizations conduct their missions/business functions; a source of threat/vulnerability information that is useful for one mission/business function could, in fact, be useful for others; or organizational guidance on assessing risk under uncertainty may be too onerous, or insufficiently defined, to be useful for one or more mission/business functions.

- *Risk response:* Information uncovered during the development of alternative courses of action could reveal that risk framing has removed or failed to uncover some potentially high-payoff alternatives from consideration. This situation may challenge organizations to revisit original assumptions or investigate ways to change established constraints.

- *Risk monitoring:* Security control monitoring by organizations could indicate that a class of controls, or a specific implementation of a control, is relatively ineffective, given investments in people, processes, or technology. This situation could lead to changes in assumptions about which types of risk responses are preferred by organizations. Monitoring of the operational environment could reveal changes in the threat landscape (e.g., changes in the tactics, techniques, and procedures observed across all organizational information systems; increasing frequency and/or intensity of attacks against specific missions/business functions) that cause organizations to revisit original threat assumptions and/or to seek different sources of threat information. Significant advances in defensive or proactive operational and technical solutions could generate the need to revisit the investment strategy identified during the framing step. Monitoring of legal/regulatory environments could also influence changes in assumptions or constraints. Also, monitoring of risk being incurred might result in the need to reconsider the organizational risk tolerance if the existing statement of risk tolerance does not appear to match the operational realities.

Activities

RISK ASSUMPTIONS

TASK 1-1: Identify assumptions that affect how risk is assessed, responded to, and monitored within the organization.

Supplemental Guidance: Organizations that identify, characterize, and provide representative examples of threat sources, vulnerabilities, consequences/impacts, and likelihood determinations promote a common terminology and frame of reference for comparing and addressing risks across disparate mission/business areas. Organizations can also select appropriate risk assessment methodologies, depending on organizational governance, culture, and how divergent the missions/business functions are within the respective organizations. For example, organizations with highly centralized governance structures might elect to use a single risk assessment methodology. Organizations with hybrid governance structures might select multiple risk assessment methodologies for Tier 2, and an additional risk assessment methodology for Tier 1 that assimilates and harmonizes the findings, results, and observations of the Tier 2 risk assessments. Alternatively, when autonomy and diversity are central to the organizational culture, organizations could define requirements for the degree of rigor and the form of results, leaving the choice of specific risk assessment methodologies to mission/business owners.

Threat Sources

Threat sources cause events having undesirable consequences or adverse impacts on organizational operations and assets, individuals, other organizations, and the Nation. Threat sources include: (i) hostile cyber/physical attacks; (ii) human errors of omission or commission; or (iii) natural and man-made disasters. For threats due to hostile cyber attacks or physical attacks, organizations provide a succinct characterization of the types of tactics, techniques, and procedures employed by adversaries that are to be addressed by safeguards and countermeasures (i.e., security controls) deployed at Tier 1 (organization level), at Tier 2 (mission/business process level), and at Tier 3 (information system level)—making explicit the types of threat-sources that are to be addressed as well as making explicit those not being addressed by the safeguards/countermeasures. Adversaries can be characterized in terms of threat levels (based on capabilities, intentions, and targeting) or with additional detail. Organizations make explicit any assumptions about threat source targeting, intentions, and capabilities. Next, organizations identify a set of representative threat events. This set of threat events provides guidance on the level of detail with which the events are described. Organizations also identify conditions for when to consider threat events in risk assessments. For example, organizations can restrict risk assessments to those threat events that have actually been observed (either internally or externally by partners or peer organizations) or alternatively, specify that threat events described by credible researchers can also be considered. Finally, organizations identify the sources of threat information found to be credible and useful (e.g., sector Information Sharing and Analysis Centers [ISACs]). Trust relationships determine from which partners, suppliers, and customers, threat information is obtained as well as the expectations placed on those partners, suppliers and customers in subsequent risk management process steps. By establishing common starting points for identifying threat sources at Tier 1, organizations provide a basis for aggregating and consolidating the results of risk assessments at Tier 2 (including risk assessments conducted for coalitions of missions and business areas or for common control providers) into an overall assessment of risk to the organization as a whole. At Tier 2, mission/business owners may identify additional sources of threat information specific to organizational missions or business functions. These sources are typically based on: (i) a particular business or critical infrastructure sector (e.g., sector ISAC); (ii) operating environments specific to the missions or lines of business (e.g., maritime, airspace); and (iii) external dependencies (e.g., GPS or satellite communications). The characterization of threat sources are refined for the missions/business functions established by organizations—with the results being that some threat sources might not be of concern, while others could be described in greater detail. At Tier 3, program managers, information system owners, and common control providers consider the phase in the system development life cycle to determine the level of detail with which threats can be considered. Greater threat specificity tends to be available later in the life cycle..

Vulnerabilities

Organizations identify approaches used to characterize vulnerabilities, consistent with the characterization of threat sources and events. Vulnerabilities can be associated with exploitable weakness or deficiencies in: (i) the hardware, software, or firmware components that compose organizational information systems (or the security controls employed within or inherited by those systems; (ii) mission/business processes and enterprise architectures (including embedded information security architectures) implemented by organizations; or (iii) organizational governance structures or processes. Vulnerabilities can also be associated with the susceptibility of organizations to adverse impacts, consequences, or harm from external sources (e.g., physical destruction of non-owned infrastructure such as electric power grids). Organizations provide guidance regarding how to consider dependencies on external organizations as vulnerabilities in the risk assessments conducted. The guidance can be informed by the types of trust relationships established by organizations with external providers. Organizations identify the degree of specificity with which vulnerabilities are described (e.g., general terms, Common Vulnerability Enumeration [CVE] identifiers, identification of weak/deficient security controls), giving some representative examples corresponding to representative threats. Organizational governance structures and processes determine how vulnerability information is shared across organizations. Organizations may also identify sources of vulnerability information found to be credible and useful. At Tier 2, mission/business owners may choose to identify additional sources of vulnerability information (e.g., a sector ISAC for information about vulnerabilities specific to that sector). At Tier 3, program managers, information system owners, and common control providers consider the phase in the system development life cycle—and in particular, the technologies included in the system – to determine the level of detail with which vulnerabilities can be considered. Organizations make explicit any assumptions about the degree of organizational or information system vulnerability to specific threat sources (by name or by type).

Consequences and Impact

Organizations provide guidance on how to assess impacts to organizational operations (i.e., mission, functions, image, and reputation), organizational assets, individuals, other organizations, and the Nation (e.g., using FIPS 199, CNSS Instruction 1253, or a more granular approach). Organizations can experience the consequences/impact of adverse events at the information system level (e.g., failing to perform as required), at the mission/business process level (e.g., failing to fully meet mission/business objectives), and at the organizational level (e.g., failing to comply with legal or regulatory requirements, damaging reputation or relationships, or undermining long-term viability). Organizations determine at Tier 1, which consequences and types of impact are to be considered at Tier 2, the mission/business process level. An adverse event can have multiple consequences and different types of impact, at different levels, and in different time frames. For example, the exposure of sensitive information (e.g., personally identifiable information) by a particular mission/business area (e.g., human resources) can have organization-wide consequences and adverse impact with regard to reputation damage; the information system consequence/impact for multiple systems of an attacker more easily overcoming identification and authentication security controls; and the mission/business process consequence/impact (for one or more mission/business areas) of an attacker falsifying information on which future decisions are based. To ensure consistency, organizations determine at Tier 1, how consequences/impacts experienced in different time frames are to be assessed. At Tier 2, mission/business owners may amplify organizational guidance, as appropriate. The types of consequences and impact considered in risk determinations are identified to provide a basis for determining, aggregating, and/or consolidating risk results and to facilitate risk communication. Organizations also provide guidance to Tier 2 and Tier 3 with regard to the extent that risk assessments are to consider the risk to other organizations and the Nation. Organization make explicit any assumptions about the degree of impact/consequences related to specific threat sources (by name or by type) or through specific vulnerabilities (individually or by type).

Likelihood

Organizations can employ a variety of approaches for determining the likelihood of threat events. Some organizations treat the likelihood that a threat event will occur and the likelihood that, if it occurs, it will result in adverse effects as separate factors, while other organizations assess threat likelihood as a combination of these factors. In addition, some organizations prefer quantitative risk assessments while other organizations, particularly when the assessment involves a high degree of uncertainty, prefer qualitative risk assessments. Likelihood determinations can be based on either threat assumptions or actual threat data (e.g., historical data on cyber attacks, historical data on earthquakes, or specific information on adversary capabilities, intentions, and targeting). When specific and credible threat data is available (e.g., types of cyber attacks, cyber attack trends, frequencies of attacks), organizations can use the empirical data and statistical analyses to determine more specific probabilities of threat events occurring. Organizations select a method consistent with organizational culture and risk tolerance. Organizations can also make explicit assumptions concerning the likelihood that a threat event will result in adverse effects as follows: (i) *worst case* (i.e., attack will be successful unless strong, objective reasons to presume otherwise); (ii) *best case* (i.e., attack will not be successful unless specific, credible information to the contrary); or (iii) something in between best and worst cases (e.g., the most probable case). Organizations document any overarching assumptions. Organizations can use empirical data and statistical analyses to help inform any of the approaches used to determine the likelihood of threat events occurring. Organizations select a method consistent with organizational culture, understanding of the operational environment, and risk tolerance.

RISK CONSTRAINTS

TASK 1-2: Identify constraints on the conduct of risk assessment, risk response, and risk monitoring activities within the organization.

Supplemental Guidance: The execution of the risk management process can be constrained in various ways, some of which are direct and obvious, while others are indirect. Financial limitations can constrain the set of risk management activities directly (e.g., by limiting the total resources available for investments in risk assessments or in safeguards or countermeasures) or indirectly (e.g., by eliminating activities which, while involving relatively small investments in risk response, entail curtailing or discarding investments in legacy information systems or information technology). Organizations might also discover that the need to continue to depend on legacy information systems may constrain the risk management options available to the organization. Constraints can also include legal, regulatory, and/or contractual requirements. Such constraints can be reflected in organizational policies (e.g., restrictions on outsourcing, restrictions on and/or requirements for information to be gathered as part of risk monitoring). Organizational culture can impose indirect constraints on governance changes (e.g., precluding a shift from decentralized to hybrid governance structures) and which security controls are considered by organizations as potential common controls. In particular, organizational attitudes toward information technology risk that, for example, favor extensive automation and early adoption of new technologies can constrain the degree of risk avoidance and perhaps risk mitigation that can be achieved. Any cultural constraints that limit senior leader/executive (e.g., chief information officer) visibility into organizational information systems that are beyond their formal authority (e.g. mission-related systems) may impede overall understanding of the complexity of information systems environment and the related risks to the organization. At Tier 2, mission/business owners interpret constraints in light of organizational missions/business functions. Some regulatory constraints may not apply to particular missions/business functions (e.g., regulations that apply to international operations, when mission/business areas are restricted to the United States). Alternately, additional requirements may apply (e.g., mission/business processes performed jointly with another organization, which imposes contractual constraints). At Tier 3, information system owners, common control providers, and/or program managers interpret the organization-wide and mission/business function-specific constraints with respect to their systems and environments of operation (e.g., requirements to provide specific security controls are satisfied through common controls).

RISK TOLERANCE

TASK 1-3: Identify the level of risk tolerance for the organization.

Supplemental Guidance: Risk tolerance is the level of risk that organizations are willing to accept in pursuit of strategic goals and objectives. Organizations define information security-related risk tolerance organization-wide considering all missions/business functions. Organizations can use a variety of techniques for identifying information security risk tolerance (e.g., by establishing zones in a likelihood-impact trade space or by using a set of representative scenarios). Organizations also define tolerance for other types of organizational and operational risks (e.g., financial, risk, safety risk, compliance risk, or reputation risk). At Tier 2, mission/business owners may have different risk tolerances from the organization as a whole. The risk executive (function) provides organizations with ways to resolve such differences in risk tolerances at Tier 2. The level of residual risk accepted by authorizing officials for information systems or inherited common controls is within the organizational risk tolerance, and not the individual risk tolerances of those authorizing officials. In addition, organizations provide to Tier 2 and Tier 3, guidance on evaluating risk for specific mission/business processes or information systems and a focus on near-term mission/business effectiveness with the longer-term, strategic focus of the organizational risk tolerance. See Section 2.3.3 for additional information on risk tolerance.

PRIORITIES AND TRADE-OFFS

TASK 1-4: Identify priorities and trade-offs considered by the organization in managing risk.

Supplemental Guidance: Risk is experienced at different levels, in different forms, and in different time frames. At Tier 1, organizations make trade-offs among and establish priorities for responding to such risks. Organizations tend to have multiple priorities that at times conflict, which generates potential risk. Approaches employed by organizations for managing portfolios of risks reflect organizational culture, risk tolerance, as well as risk-related assumptions and constraints. These approaches are typically embodied in the strategic plans, policies, and roadmaps of organizations which may indicate preferences for different forms of risk response. For example, organizations may be willing to accept short-term risk of slightly degraded operations to achieve long-term reduction in information security risk. However, this trade-off could be unacceptable for one particularly critical mission/business function (e.g., real-time requirements in many industrial/process control systems). For that high-priority area, a different approach to improving security may be required including the application of compensating security controls.

Outputs and Post Conditions

The output of the risk framing step is the *risk management strategy* that identifies how organizations intend to assess, respond to, and monitor risk over time. The framing step also produces a set of organizational policies, procedures, standards, guidance, and resources covering the following topics: (i) scope of the organizational risk management process (e.g., organizational entities covered; mission/business functions affected; how risk management activities are applied within the risk management tiers); (ii) risk assessment guidance including, for example, the characterization of threat sources, sources of threat information, representative threat events (in particular, adversary tactics, techniques, and procedures), when to consider and how to evaluate threats, sources of vulnerability information, risk assessment methodologies to be used, and risk assumptions; (iii) risk response guidance including, for example, risk tolerances, risk response concepts to be employed, opportunity costs, trade-offs, consequences of responses, hierarchy of authorities, and priorities; (iv) risk monitoring guidance, including, for example, guidance on analysis of monitored risk factors to determine changes in risk, and monitoring frequency, methods, and reporting; (v) other and risk constraints on executing risk management activities; and (vi) organizational priorities and trade-offs. Outputs from the risk framing step serve as inputs to the risk assessment, risk response, and risk monitoring steps.

3.2 ASSESSING RISK

Risk assessment identifies, prioritizes, and estimates risk to organizational operations (i.e., mission, functions, image, and reputation), organizational assets, individuals, other organizations, and the Nation, resulting from the operation and use of information systems.[62] Risk assessments use the results of threat and vulnerability assessments to identify and evaluate risk in terms of likelihood of occurrence and potential adverse impact (i.e., magnitude of harm) to organizations, assets, and individuals. Risk assessments can be conducted at any of the risk management tiers

---

[62] Draft NIST Special Publication 800-30, Revision 1, provides guidance on conducting risk assessments (including incremental or differential risk assessments) across all three tiers in the multitiered risk management approach.

with different objectives and utility of the information produced. For example, risk assessments conducted at Tier 1 or Tier 2 focus on organizational operations, assets, and individuals—whether comprehensive across mission/business lines or only on those assessments that are cross-cutting to the particular mission/business line. Organization-wide assessments of risk can be based solely on the assumptions, constraints, risk tolerances, priorities, and trade-offs established in the risk framing step (derived primarily from Tier 1 activities) or can be based on risk assessments conducted across multiple mission/business lines (derived primarily from Tier 2 activities). Risk assessments conducted at one tier can be used to refine/enhance threat, vulnerability, likelihood, and impact information used in assessments conducted in other tiers. The degree that information from risk assessments can be reused is shaped by the similarity of missions/business functions and the degree of autonomy that organizational entities or subcomponents have with respect to parent organizations. Organizations that are decentralized can expect to conduct more risk assessment activities at Tier 2 and, as a result, may have a greater need to communicate within Tier 2 to identify cross-cutting threats and vulnerabilities. Decentralized organizations can still benefit from Tier 1 risk assessments and, in particular, the identification of an initial set of threat and vulnerability sources. Organization-wide risk assessments provide some initial prioritization of risks for decision makers to consider when entering the risk response step.

Organizations benefit significantly from conducting risk assessments as part of an organization-wide risk management process. However, once risk assessments are complete, it is prudent for organizations to invest some time in keeping the assessments current. Maintaining currency of risk assessments requires support from the risk monitoring step (e.g., observing changes in organizational information systems and environments of operation or analyzing monitoring results to maintain awareness of the risk). Keeping risk assessments up to date provides many potential benefits such as timely, relevant information that enables senior leaders/executives to perform near real-time risk management. Maintaining risk assessments also reduces future assessment costs and supports ongoing risk monitoring efforts. Organizations may determine that conducting comprehensive risk assessments as a way of maintaining current risk assessments do not provide sufficient value. In such situations, organizations consider conducting incremental and/or differential risk assessments. Incremental risk assessments consider only new information (e.g., the effects of using a new information system on mission/business risk), whereas differential risk assessments consider how changes affect the overall risk determination. Incremental or differential risk assessments are useful if organizations require a more targeted review of risk, seek an expanded understanding of risk, or desire an expanded understanding of the risk in relation to missions/business functions.

STEP 2: RISK ASSESSMENT

Inputs and Preconditions

Inputs to the risk assessment step from the risk framing step include, for example: (i) acceptable risk assessment methodologies; (ii) the breadth and depth of analysis employed during risk assessments; (iii) the level of granularity required for describing threats; (iv) whether/how to assess external service providers; and (v) whether/how to aggregate risk assessment results from different organizational entities or mission/business functions to the organization as a whole. Organizational expectations regarding risk assessment methodologies, techniques, and/or procedures are shaped heavily by governance structures, risk tolerance, culture, trust, and life cycle processes. Prior to conducting risk assessments, organizations understand the fundamental reasons for conducting the assessments and what constitutes adequate depth and breadth for the assessments. Risk assumptions, risk constraints, risk tolerance, and priorities/trade-offs defined during the risk framing step shape how organizations use risk assessments—for example, localized applications of the risk assessments within each of the risk management tiers (i.e., governance, mission/business process, information systems) or global applications of the risk assessments across the entire organization. Risk assessments can be conducted by organizations even when some of the inputs from the risk framing step have not been received or preconditions established. However, in those situations, the quality of the risk assessment results may be affected. In addition to the risk framing step, the risk assessment step can receive inputs from the risk monitoring step, especially during mission operations and the operations/maintenance phase of the system development life cycle (e.g., when organizations discover new threats or vulnerabilities that require an immediate reassessment of risk). The risk assessment step can also receive inputs from the risk response step (e.g., when organizations are considering the risk of employing new technology-based solutions as alternatives for risk reduction measures). As courses of action are developed in the risk response step, a differential risk assessment may be needed to evaluate differences that each course of action makes in the overall risk determination.

Activities

THREAT AND VULNERABILITY IDENTIFICATION

TASK 2-1: Identify threats to and vulnerabilities in organizational information systems and the environments in which the systems operate.

Supplemental Guidance: Threat identification requires an examination of threat sources and events. For examining threat sources and events, organizations identify threat capabilities, intentions, and targeting information from all available sources. Organizations can leverage a number of sources for threat information at strategic or tactical levels. Threat information generated at any tier can be used to inform or refine the risk-related activities in any other tier. For example, specific threats (i.e., tactics, techniques, and procedures) identified during Tier 1 threat assessments may directly affect mission/business process and architectural design decisions at Tier 2. Specific threat information generated at Tiers 2 and 3 can be used by organizations to refine threat information generated during initial threat assessments carried out at Tier 1.

Vulnerability identification occurs at all tiers. Vulnerabilities related to organizational governance (e.g., inconsistent decisions about the relative priorities of mission/business processes, selection of incompatible implementations of security controls) as well as vulnerabilities related to external dependencies (e.g., electrical power, supply chain, telecommunications), are most effectively identified at Tier 1. However, most vulnerability identification occurs at Tiers 2 and 3. At Tier 2, process and architecture-related vulnerabilities (e.g., exploitable weaknesses or deficiencies in mission/business processes, enterprise /information security architectures including embedded information security architectures) are more likely to be identified. At Tier 3, information system vulnerabilities are the primary focus. These vulnerabilities are commonly found in the hardware, software, and firmware components of information systems or in the environments in which the systems operate. Other areas of potential vulnerabilities include vulnerabilities associated with the definition, application/implementation, and monitoring of processes, procedures and services related to management, operational, and technical aspects of information security. Vulnerabilities associated with architectural design and mission/business processes can have a greater impact on the ability of organizations to successfully carry out missions and business functions due to the potential impact across multiple information systems and mission environments. The refined vulnerability assessments conducted at Tiers 2 and 3 are shared with organizational personnel responsible for assessing risks more strategically. Vulnerability assessments conducted at Tier 2 and Tier 3 have the opportunity to evaluate additional related variables such as location, proximity to other high risk assets (physical or logical), and resource considerations related to operational environments. Information specific to operational environments allows for more useful and actionable assessment results. Vulnerability identification can be accomplished at a per-individual weakness/deficiency level or at a root-cause level. When selecting between approaches, organizations consider whether the overall objective is identifying each specific instance or symptom of a problem or understanding the underlying root causes of problems. Understanding specific exploitable weaknesses or deficiencies is helpful when problems are first identified or when quick fixes are required. This specific understanding also provides organizations with necessary sources of information for eventually diagnosing potential root causes of problems, especially those problems that are systemic in nature.

Organizations with more established enterprise architectures (including embedded information security architectures) and mature life cycle processes have outputs that can be used to inform risk assessment processes. Risk assumptions, constraints, tolerances, priorities, and trade-offs used for developing enterprise architectures and embedded information security architectures can be useful sources of information for initial risk assessment activities. Risk assessments conducted to support the development of segment or solution architectures may also serve as information sources for the identification of threats and vulnerabilities. Another factor influencing threat and vulnerability identification is organizational culture. Organizations that promote free and open communications and non-retribution for sharing adverse information tend to foster greater openness from individuals working within those organizations. Frequently, organizational personnel operating at Tiers 2 and 3 have valuable information and can make meaningful contributions in the area of threat and vulnerability identification. The culture of organizations influences the willingness of personnel to communicate potential threat and vulnerability information, which ultimately affects the quality and quantity of the threats/vulnerabilities identified.

RISK DETERMINATION

TASK 2-2: Determine the risk to organizational operations and assets, individuals, other organizations, and the Nation if identified threats exploit identified vulnerabilities.

Supplemental Guidance: Organizations determine risk by considering the likelihood that known threats exploit known vulnerabilities and the resulting consequences or adverse impacts (i.e., magnitude of harm) if such exploitations occur. Organizations use threat and vulnerability information together with likelihood and consequences/impact information to determine risk either qualitatively or quantitatively. Organizations can employ a variety of approaches to determine the likelihood of threats exploiting vulnerabilities. Likelihood determinations can be based on either threat assumptions or actual threat information (e.g., historical data on cyber attacks, historical data on earthquakes, or specific information on adversary capabilities, intentions, and targeting). When specific and credible threat information is available (e.g., types of cyber attacks, cyber attack trends, frequencies of attacks), organizations can use empirical data and statistical analyses to determine more specific probabilities of threats occurring. Assessment of likelihood can also be influenced by whether vulnerability identification occurred at the individual weakness or deficiency level or at the root-cause level. The relative ease/difficulty of vulnerability exploitation, the sophistication of adversaries, and the nature of operational environments all influence the likelihood that threats exploit vulnerabilities. Organizations can characterize adverse impacts by security objective (e.g., loss of confidentiality, integrity, or availability). However, to maximize usefulness, adverse impact is expressed in or translated into terms of organizational missions, business functions, and stakeholders.

Risk Determination and Uncertainty

Risk determinations require analysis of threat, vulnerability, likelihood, and impact-related information. Organizations also need to examine mission/business vulnerabilities and threats where safeguards and/or countermeasures do not exist. The nature of the inputs provided to this step (e.g., general, specific, strategic, tactical) directly affects the type of outputs or risk determinations made. The reliability and accuracy of risk determinations are dependent on the currency, accuracy, completeness, and integrity of information collected to support the risk assessment process. In addition, the components of risk assessment results that affect reliability and accuracy of risk determinations also affect the amount of uncertainty associated with those risk determinations and subsequent determinations. Organizations also consider additional insights related to the anticipated time frames associated with particular risks. Time horizons associated with potential threats can shape future risk responses (e.g., risk may not be a concern if the time horizon for the risk is in the distant future).

Organizational guidance for determining risk under uncertainty indicates how combinations of likelihood and impact are combined into a determination of the risk level or risk score/rating. Organizations need to understand the type and amount of uncertainty surrounding risk decisions so that risk determinations can be understood. During the risk framing step, organizations may have provided guidance on how to analyze risk and how to determine risk when a high degree of uncertainty exists. Uncertainty is particularly a concern when the risk assessment considers advanced persistent threats, for which analysis of interacting vulnerabilities may be needed, the common body of knowledge is sparse, and past behavior may not be predictive.

While threat and vulnerability determinations apply frequently to missions and business functions, the specific requirements associated with the missions/business functions, including the environments of operation, may lead to different assessment results. Different missions, business functions, and environments of operation can lead to differences in the applicability of specific threat information considered and the likelihood of threats causing potential harm. Understanding the threat component of the risk assessment requires insight into the particular threats facing specific missions or business functions. Such awareness of threats includes understanding the capability, intent, and targeting of particular adversaries. The risk tolerance of organizations and underlying beliefs associated with how the risk tolerance is formed (including the culture within organizations) may shape the perception of impact and likelihood in the context of identified threats and vulnerabilities.

Even with the establishment of explicit criteria, risk assessments are influenced by organizational culture and the personal experiences and accumulated knowledge of the individuals conducting the assessments. As a result, assessors of risk can reach different conclusions from the same information. This diversity of perspective can enrich the risk assessment process and provide decision makers with a greater array of information and potentially fewer biases. However, such diversity may also lead to risk assessments that are inconsistent. Organizationally-defined and applied processes provide the means to identify inconsistent practices and include processes to identify and resolve such inconsistencies.

Outputs and Post Conditions

The output of the risk assessment step is a determination of risk to organizational operations (i.e., mission, functions, image, and reputation), organizational assets, individuals, other organizations, and the Nation. Depending on the approach that organizations take, either the overall risk to the organization or the inputs used to determine risk may be communicated to the decision makers responsible for risk response. In certain situations, there are recurring cycles between the risk assessment step and the risk response step until particular objectives are achieved. Based on the course of action selected during the risk response step, some residual risk may remain. Under certain circumstances, the level of residual risk could trigger a reassessment of risk. This reassessment is typically incremental (assessing only the new information) and differential (assessing how the new information changes the overall risk determination).

The aggregation of risk assessment results from all three tiers drives the management of portfolios of risks undertaken by organizations. Identified risks common to more than one mission/business function within organizations may also be the source for future assessment activities at Tier 1, such as root-cause analysis. Gaining a better understanding of the reasons why certain risks are more common or frequent assists decision makers in selecting risk responses that address underlying (or root-cause) problems instead of solely focusing on the surface issues surrounding the existence of the risks. The results of risk assessments can also shape future design and development decisions related to enterprise architecture (including embedded information security architecture), and organizational information systems. The extent to which missions/business functions are vulnerable to a set of identified threats and the relative ease with which those vulnerabilities can be exploited, contribute to the risk-related information provided to senior leaders/executives.

Outputs from the risk assessment step can be useful inputs to the risk framing and risk monitoring steps. For example, risk determinations can result in revisiting the organizational risk tolerance established during the risk framing step. Organizations can also choose to use information from the risk assessment step to inform the risk monitoring step. For example, risk assessments can include recommendations to monitor specific elements of risk (e.g., threat sources) so that if certain thresholds are crossed, previous risk assessment results can be reviewed and updated, as appropriate. Particular thresholds established as part of risk monitoring programs can also serve as the basis for reassessments of risk. If organizations establish criteria as a part of the risk framing step for when risk assessment results do not warrant risk responses, then assessment results could be fed directly to the risk monitoring step as a source of input.

3.3 RESPONDING TO RISK

Risk response identifies, evaluates, decides on, and implements appropriate courses of action to accept, avoid, mitigate, share, or transfer risk to organizational operations and assets, individuals, other organizations, and the Nation, resulting from the operation and use of information systems. Identifying and analyzing alternative courses of action[63] typically occurs at Tier 1 or Tier 2. This is due to the fact that alternative courses of action (i.e., potential risk responses) are evaluated in terms of anticipated organization-wide impacts and the ability of organizations to continue to successfully carry out organizational missions and business functions. Decisions to employ risk response measures organization-wide are typically made at Tier 1, although the decisions are informed by risk-related information from the lower tiers. At Tier 2, alternative courses of action are evaluated in terms of anticipated impacts on organizational missions/business functions, the associated mission/business processes supporting the missions/business functions, and resource requirements. At Tier 3, alternative courses of action tend to be evaluated in terms of the system development life cycle or the maximum amount of time available for implementing the selected course(s) of action. The breadth of potential risk responses is a major factor for whether the activity is carried out at Tier 1, Tier 2, or Tier 3. Risk decisions are influenced by organizational risk tolerance developed as part of risk framing activities at Tier 1. Organizations can implement risk decisions at any of the risk management tiers with different objectives and utility of information produced.

STEP 3: RISK RESPONSE

Inputs and Preconditions

Inputs from the risk assessment and risk framing steps include: (i) identification of threat sources and threat events; (ii) identification of vulnerabilities that are subject to exploitation; (iii) estimates of potential consequences and/or impact if

---

[63] A *course of action* is a time-phased or situation-dependent combination of risk response measures. A *risk response measure* is a specific action taken to respond to an identified risk. Risk response measures can be separately managed and can include, for example, the implementation of security controls to mitigate risk, promulgation of security policies to avoid risk or to accept risk in specific circumstances, and organizational agreements to share or transfer risk.

threats exploit vulnerabilities; (iv) likelihood estimates that threats exploit vulnerabilities; (v) a determination of risk to organizational operations (i.e., mission, functions, image, and reputation), organizational assets, individuals, other organizations, and the Nation; (vi) risk response guidance from the organizational risk management strategy (see Appendix H); and (vii) the general organizational directions and guidance on appropriate responses to risk. In addition to the risk assessment and risk framing steps, the risk response step can receive inputs from the risk monitoring step (e.g., when organizations experience a breach or compromise to their information systems or environments of operation that require an immediate response to address the incident and reduce additional risk that results from the event). The risk response step can also receive inputs from the risk framing step (e.g., when organizations are required to deploy new safeguards and countermeasures in their information systems based on security requirements in new legislation or OMB policies). The risk framing step also directly shapes the resource constraints associated with selecting an appropriate course of action. Additional preconditions established at the risk framing step may include: (i) constraints based on architecture and previous investments; (ii) organizational preferences and tolerances; (iii) the expected effectiveness at mitigating risk (including how effectiveness is measured and monitored); and (iv) the time horizon for the risk (e.g., current risk, projected risk—that is, a risk expected to arise in the future based on the results of threat assessments or a planned changes in missions/business functions, enterprise architecture (including information security architecture), or aspects of legal or regulatory compliance).

Activities

RISK RESPONSE IDENTIFICATION

TASK 3-1: Identify alternative courses of action to respond to risk determined during the risk assessment.

Supplemental Guidance: Organizations can respond to risk in a variety of ways. These include: (i) risk acceptance; (ii) risk avoidance; (iii) risk mitigation; (iv) risk sharing; (v) risk transfer; or (vi) a combination of the above. A course of action is a time-phased or situation-dependent combination of risk response measures. For example, in an emergency situation, organizations might accept the risk associated with unfiltered connection to an external communications provider for a limited time; then avoid risk by cutting the connection; mitigate risk in the near-term by applying security controls to search for malware or evidence of unauthorized access to information that occurred during the period of unfiltered connection; and finally mitigate risk long-term by applying controls to handle such connections more securely.

Risk Acceptance

Risk acceptance is the appropriate risk response when the identified risk is within the organizational risk tolerance. Organizations can accept risk deemed to be low, moderate, or high depending on particular situations or conditions. For example, organizations with data centers residing in the northeastern portion of the United States may opt to accept the risk of earthquakes based on known likelihood of earthquakes and data center vulnerability to damage by earthquakes. Organizations accept the fact that earthquakes are possible, but given the infrequency of major earthquakes in that region of the country, believe it is not cost-effective to address such risk—that is, the organizations have determined that risk associated with earthquakes is low. Conversely, organizations may accept substantially greater risk (in the moderate/high range) due to compelling mission, business, or operational needs. For example, federal agencies may decide to share very sensitive information with first responders who do not typically have access to such information due to time-sensitive needs to stop pending terrorist attacks, even though the information is not itself perishable with regard to risk through loss of confidentiality. Organizations typically make determinations regarding the general level of acceptable risk and the types of acceptable risk with consideration of organizational priorities and trade-offs between: (i) near-term mission/business needs and potential for longer-term mission/business impacts; and (ii) organizational interests and the potential impacts on individuals, other organizations, and the Nation.

Risk Avoidance

Risk avoidance may be the appropriate risk response when the identified risk exceeds the organizational risk tolerance. Organizations may conduct certain types of activities or employ certain types of information technologies that result in risk that is unacceptable. In such situations, risk avoidance involves taking specific actions to eliminate the activities or technologies that are the basis for the risk or to revise or reposition these activities or technologies in the organizational mission/business processes to avoid the potential for unacceptable risk. For example, organizations planning to employ networked connections between two domains, may determine through risk assessments that there is unacceptable risk in establishing such connections. Organizations may also determine that implementing effective safeguards and countermeasures (e.g., cross-domain solutions) is not practical in the given circumstances. Thus, the organizations decide to avoid the risk by eliminating the electronic or networked connections and employing an "air gap" with a manual connection processes (e.g., data transfers by secondary storage devices).

Risk Mitigation

Risk mitigation, or risk reduction, is the appropriate risk response for that portion of risk that cannot be accepted, avoided, shared, or transferred. The alternatives to mitigate risk depend on: (i) the risk management tier and the scope of risk response decisions assigned or delegated to organizational officials at that tier (defined by the organizational governance structures); and (ii) the organizational risk management strategy and associated risk response strategies. The means used by organizations to mitigate risk can involve a combination of risk response measures across the three tiers. For example, risk mitigation can include common security controls at Tier 1, process re-engineering at Tier 2, and/or new or enhanced management, operational, or technical safeguards or countermeasures (or some combination of all three) at Tier 3. Another example of a potential risk requiring mitigation can be illustrated when adversaries gain access to mobile devices (e.g., laptop computers or personal digital assistants) while users are traveling. Possible risk mitigation measures include, for example, organizational policies prohibiting transport of mobile devices to certain areas of the world or procedures for users to obtain a clean mobile device that is never allowed to connect to the organizational networks.

Risk Sharing or Transfer

Risk sharing or risk transfer is the appropriate risk response when organizations desire and have the means to shift risk liability and responsibility to other organizations. Risk transfer shifts the entire risk responsibility or liability from one organization to another organization (e.g., using insurance to transfer risk from particular organizations to insurance companies). Risk sharing shifts a portion of risk responsibility or liability to other organizations (usually organizations that are more qualified to address the risk). It is important to note that risk transfer reduces neither the likelihood of harmful events occurring nor the consequences in terms of harm to organizational operations and assets, individuals, other organizations, or the Nation. Risk sharing may be a sharing of liability or a sharing of responsibility for other, adequate risk responses such as mitigation. Therefore, the concept of risk transfer is less applicable in the public sector (e.g., federal, state, local governments) than the private sector, as liability of organizations is generally established by legislation or policy. As such, self-initiated transfers of risk by public sector organizations (as typified by purchasing insurance) are generally not possible. Risk sharing often occurs when organizations determine that addressing risk requires expertise or resources that are better provided by other organizations. For example, an identified risk might be the physical penetration of perimeters and kinetic attacks by terrorist groups. The organization decides to partner with another organization sharing the physical facility to take joint responsibility for addressing risk from kinetic attacks.

EVALUATION OF ALTERNATIVES

TASK 3-2: Evaluate alternative courses of action for responding to risk.

Supplemental Guidance: The evaluation of alternative courses of action can include: (i) the expected effectiveness in achieving desired risk response (and how effectiveness is measured and monitored); and (ii) anticipated feasibility of implementation, including, for example, mission/business impact, political, legal, social, financial, technical, and economic considerations. Economic considerations include costs throughout the expected period of time during which the course of action is followed (e.g., cost of procurement, integration into organizational processes at Tier 1 and/or Tier 2, information systems at Tier 3, training, and maintenance). During the evaluation of alternative courses of action, trade-offs can be made explicit between near-term gains in mission/business effectiveness or efficiency and long-term risk of mission/business harm due to compromise of information or information systems that are providing this near-term benefit. For example, organizations concerned about the potential for mobile devices (e.g., laptop computers) being compromised while employees are on travel can evaluate several courses of action including: (i) providing users traveling to high-risk areas with clean laptops; (ii) removing hard drives from laptops and operate from CDs or DVDs; or (iii) having laptops go through a detailed assessment before being allowed to connect to organizational networks. The first option is highly effective as returning laptops are never connected to organizational networks. While the second option ensures that hard drives cannot be corrupted, it is not quite as effective in that it is still possible that hardware devices (e.g., motherboards) could have been compromised. The effectiveness of the third option is limited by the ability of organizations to detect potential insertion of malware into the hardware, firmware, or software. As such, it is the least effective of the three options. From a cost perspective, the first option is potentially the most expensive, depending upon the number of travelers (hence number of travel laptops) required. The second and third options are considerably less expensive. From a mission and operational perspective, the third option is the best alternative as users have access to standard laptop configurations including all applications and supporting data needed to perform tasks supporting missions and business functions. Such applications and data would not be available if the first or second option is selected. Ultimately, the evaluation of courses of action is made based on operational requirements, including information security requirements, needed for near and long term mission/business success. Budgetary constraints, consistency with investment management strategies, civil liberties, and privacy protection, are some of the important elements organizations consider when selecting appropriate courses of action. In those instances where organizations only identify a single course of action, then the evaluation is focused on whether the course of action is adequate. If the course of action is deemed inadequate, then organizations need to refine the identified course of action to address the inadequacies or develop another course of action (see Task 3-1).

In summary, a risk verses risk-response trade-off is conducted for each course of action to provide the information necessary for: (i) selecting between the courses of action; and (ii) evaluating the courses of action in terms of response effectiveness, costs, mission/business impact, and any other factors deemed relevant to organizations. Part of risk versus risk-response trade-off considers the issue of competing resources. From an organizational perspective, this means organizations consider whether the cost (e.g., money, personnel, time) for implementing a given course of action has the potential to adversely impact other missions or business functions, and if so, to what extent. This is necessary because organizations have finite resources to employ and many competing missions/business functions across many organizational elements. Therefore, organizations assess the overall value of alternative courses of action with regard to the missions/business functions and the potential risk to each organizational element. Organizations may determine that irrespective of a particular mission/business function and the validity of the associated risk, there are more important missions/business functions that face more significant risks, and hence have a better claim on the limited resources.

RISK RESPONSE DECISION

TASK 3-3: Decide on the appropriate course of action for responding to risk.

Supplemental Guidance: Decisions on the most appropriate course of action include some form of prioritization. Some risks may be of greater concern than other risks. In that case, more resources may need to be directed at addressing higher-priority risks than at other lower-priority risks. This does not necessarily mean that the lower-priority risks would not be addressed. Rather, it could mean that fewer resources might be directed at the lower-priority risks (at least initially), or that the lower-priority risks would be addressed at a later time. A key part of the risk decision process is the recognition that regardless of the decision, there still remains a degree of residual risk that must be addressed. Organizations determine acceptable degrees of residual risk based on organizational risk tolerance and the specific risk tolerances of particular decision makers. Impacting the decision process are some of the more intangible risk-related concepts (e.g., risk tolerance, trust, and culture). The specific beliefs and approaches that organizations embrace with respect to these risk-related concepts affect the course of action selected by decision-makers.

RISK RESPONSE IMPLEMENTATION

TASK 3-4: Implement the course of action selected to respond to risk.

Supplemental Guidance: Once a course of action is selected, organizations implement the associated risk response. Given the size and complexity of some organizations, the actual implementation of risk response measures may be challenging. Some risk response measures are tactical in nature (e.g., applying patches to identified vulnerabilities in organizational information systems) and may be implemented rather quickly. Other risk response measures may be more strategic in nature and reflect solutions that take much longer to implement. Therefore, organizations apply, and tailor as appropriate to a specific risk response course of action, the risk response implementation considerations in the risk response strategies (part of the risk management strategy developed during the risk framing step). See Appendix H, Risk Response Strategies.

Outputs and Post Conditions

The output of the risk response step is the implementation of the selected courses of action with consideration for: (i) individuals or organizational elements responsible for the selected risk response measures and specifications of effectiveness criteria (i.e., articulation of indicators and thresholds against which the effectiveness of risk response measures can be judged); (ii) dependencies of each selected risk response measure on other risk response measures; (iii) dependencies of selected risk response measures on other factors (e.g., the implementation of other planned information technology measures); (iv) timeline for implementation of risk response measures; (v) plans for monitoring the effectiveness of risk response measures; (vi) identification of risk monitoring triggers; and (vii) interim risk response measures selected for implementation, if appropriate. There are also ongoing communications and sharing of risk-related information with individuals or organizational elements impacted by the risk responses (including potential actions that may need to be taken by the individuals or organizational elements).

In addition to the risk monitoring step, outputs from the risk response step can be useful inputs to the risk framing and risk assessment steps. For example, it is possible that the analysis occurring during the evaluation of alternative courses of action may call into question some aspects of the risk response strategy that is part of the risk management strategy generated during the risk framing step. In such instances, organizations use that information to inform the risk framing step with appropriate actions taken to revisit the risk management strategy and its associated risk response strategy. Organizations might also determine during the evaluation of alternative courses of action for risk response, that some aspects of the risk assessments are incomplete or incorrect. This information can be used to inform the risk assessment step possibly resulting in further analysis or reassessments of risk.

3.4 MONITORING RISK

Risk monitoring provides organizations with the means to: (i) verify *compliance*;[64] (ii) determine the ongoing *effectiveness* of risk response measures; and (iii) identify risk-impacting *changes* to organizational information systems and environments of operation. Analyzing monitoring results gives organizations the capability to maintain awareness of the risk being incurred, highlight the need to revisit other steps in the risk management process, and initiate process improvement activities as needed.[65] Organizations employ risk monitoring tools, techniques, and procedures to increase risk awareness, helping senior leaders/executives develop a better understanding of the ongoing risk to organizational operations and assets, individuals, other organizations, and the Nation. Organizations can implement risk monitoring at any of the risk management tiers with different objectives and utility of information produced. For example, Tier 1 monitoring activities might include ongoing threat assessments and how changes in the threat space may affect Tier 2 and Tier 3 activities, including enterprise architectures (with embedded information security architectures) and organizational information systems. Tier 2 monitoring activities might include, for example, analyses of new or current technologies either in use or considered for future use by organizations to identify exploitable weaknesses and/or deficiencies in those technologies that may affect mission/business success. Tier 3 monitoring activities focus on information systems and might include, for example, automated monitoring of standard configuration settings for information technology products, vulnerability scanning, and ongoing assessments of security controls. In addition to deciding on appropriate monitoring activities across the risk management tiers, organizations also decide how monitoring is to be conducted (e.g., automated or manual approaches) and the frequency of monitoring activities based on, for example, the frequency with which deployed security controls change, critical items on plans of action and milestones, and risk tolerance.

STEP 4: RISK MONITORING

Inputs and Preconditions

Inputs to this step include implementation strategies for selected courses of action for risk responses and the actual implementation of selected courses of action. In addition to the risk response step, the risk monitoring step can receive inputs from the risk framing step (e.g., when organizations become aware of an advanced persistent threat reflecting a change in threat assumptions, this may result in a change in the frequency of follow on monitoring activities). The risk framing step also directly shapes the resource constraints associated with establishing and implementing an organization-wide monitoring strategy. In some instances, outputs from the risk assessment step may be useful inputs to the risk monitoring step. For example, risk assessment threshold conditions (e.g., likelihood of threats exploiting vulnerabilities) could be input to the risk monitoring step. In turn, organizations could monitor to determine if such threshold conditions are met. If threshold conditions are met, such information could be used in the risk assessment step, where it could serve as the basis for an incremental, differential risk assessment or an overall reassessment of risk to the organization.

Activities

RISK MONITORING STRATEGY

TASK 4-1: Develop a risk monitoring strategy for the organization that includes the purpose, type, and frequency of monitoring activities.

---

[64] Compliance verification ensures that organizations have implemented required risk response measures and that information security requirements derived from and traceable to organizational missions/business functions, federal legislation, directives, regulations, policies, and standards/guidelines are satisfied.

[65] Draft NIST Special Publication 800-137 provides guidance on monitoring organizational information systems and environments of operation.

Supplemental Guidance: Organizations implement risk monitoring programs: (i) to verify that required risk response measures are implemented and that information security requirements derived from and traceable to organizational missions/business functions, federal legislation, directives, regulations, policies, and standards/guidelines, are satisfied (*compliance monitoring*); (ii) to determine the ongoing effectiveness of risk response measures after the measures have been implemented (*effectiveness monitoring*); and (iii) to identify changes to organizational information systems and the environments in which the systems operate that may affect risk (*change monitoring*) including changes in the feasibility of the ongoing implementation of risk response measures). Determining the purpose of risk monitoring programs directly impacts the means used by organizations to conduct the monitoring activities and where monitoring occurs (i.e., at which risk management tiers). Organizations also determine the type of monitoring to be employed, including approaches that rely on automation or approaches that rely on procedural/manual activities with human intervention. Finally, organizations determine how often monitoring activities are conducted, balancing value gained from frequent monitoring with potential for operational disruptions due for example, to interruption of mission/business processes, reduction in operational bandwidth during monitoring, and shift of resources from operations to monitoring. Monitoring strategies developed at Tier 1 influence and provide direction for similar strategies developed at Tier 2 and Tier 3 including the monitoring activities associated with the Risk Management Framework at the information system level.

Monitoring Compliance

Compliance monitoring is employed to ensure that organizations are implementing needed risk response measures. This includes ensuring that the risk response measures selected and implemented by organizations in response to risk determinations produced from risk assessments are implemented correctly and operating as intended. Failure to implement the risk response measures selected by organizations can result in the organizations continuing to be subject to the identified risk. Compliance monitoring also includes ensuring that risk response measures required by federal mandates (e.g., legislation, directives, policies, regulations, standards) or organizational mandates (e.g., local policies, procedures, mission/business requirements) are implemented. Compliance monitoring is the easiest type of monitoring to perform because there are typically a finite set of risk response measures employed by organizations usually in the form of security controls. Such measures are typically well-defined and articulated as an output from the risk response step. The more challenging part of compliance monitoring is evaluating whether the risk response measures are implemented correctly (and in some instances continuously). Compliance monitoring also includes, as feasible, analysis as to why compliance failed. The reason for compliance failure can range from individuals failing to do their jobs correctly to the risk response measure not functioning as intended. If monitoring indicates a failure in compliance, then the response step of the risk management process is revisited. A key element of the feedback to the response step is the finding from compliance monitoring indicating the reason for the compliance failure. In some instances, compliance failures can be fixed by simply re-implementing the same risk response measures with little or no change. But in other instances, compliance failures are more complicated (e.g., the selected risk response measures are too difficult to implement or the measures did not function as expected). In such instances, it may be necessary for organizations to return to the evaluation and decision portions of the risk response step to develop different risk response measures.

Monitoring Effectiveness

Effectiveness monitoring is employed by organizations to determine if implemented risk response measures have actually been effective in reducing identified risk to the desired level. Although effectiveness monitoring is different than compliance monitoring, failure to achieve desired levels of effectiveness may be an indication that risk response measures have been implemented incorrectly or are not operating as intended. Determining the effectiveness of risk response measures is generally more challenging than determining whether the measures have been implemented correctly and are operating as intended (i.e., meeting identified compliance requirements). Risk response measures implemented correctly and operating as intended do not guarantee an effective reduction of risk. This is primarily due to: (i) the complexity of operating environments which may generate unintended consequences; (ii) subsequent changes in levels of risk or associated risk factors (e.g., threats, vulnerabilities, impact, or likelihood); (iii) inappropriate or incomplete criteria established as an output of the risk response step; and (iv) changes in information systems and environments of operation after implementation of risk response measures. This is especially true when organizations try to determine if more strategic outcomes have been achieved and for more dynamic operating environments. For example, if the desired outcome for organizations is to be less susceptible to advanced persistent threats, this may be challenging to measure since these types of threats are, by definition, very difficult to detect. Even when organizations are able to establish effectiveness criteria, it is often difficult to obtain criteria that are quantifiable. Therefore, it may become a matter of subjective judgment as to whether the implemented risk response measures are ultimately effective. Moreover, even if quantifiable effectiveness criteria are provided, it may be difficult to determine if the information provided satisfies the criteria. If organizations determine that risk response measures are not effective, then it may be necessary to return to the risk response step. Generally, for effectiveness failures, organizations cannot simply return to the implementation portion of the risk response step. Therefore, depending on the reason for the lack of effectiveness, organizations revisit all portions of the risk response step (i.e., development, evaluation, decision, and implementation) and potentially the risk assessment step. These activities may result in organizations developing and implementing entirely new risk responses.

Monitoring Changes

In addition to compliance monitoring and effectiveness monitoring, organizations monitor changes to organizational information systems and the environments in which those systems operate. Monitoring changes to information systems and environments of operation is not linked directly to previous risk response measures but it is nonetheless important to detect changes that may affect the risk to organizational operations and assets, individuals, other organizations, and the Nation. Generally, such monitoring detects changes in conditions that may undermine risk assumptions (articulated in the risk framing step).

- *Information System:* Changes can occur in organizational information systems (including hardware, software, and firmware) that can introduce new risk or change existing risk. For example, updates to operating system software can eliminate security capabilities that existed in earlier versions, thus introducing new vulnerabilities into organizational information systems. Another example is the discovery of new system vulnerabilities that fall outside of the scope of the tools and processes available to address such vulnerabilities (e.g., vulnerabilities for which there are no established mitigations).

- *Environments of Operation:* The environments in which information systems operate can also change in ways that introduce new risk or change existing risk. Environmental and operational considerations include, but are not limited to, missions/business functions, threats, vulnerabilities, mission/business processes, facilities, policies, legislation, and technologies. For example, new legislation or regulations could be passed that impose additional requirements on organizations. This change might affect the risk assumptions established by organizations. Another example is a change in the threat environment that reports new tactics, techniques, procedures, or increases in the technical capabilities of adversaries. Organizations might experience reductions in available resources (e.g., personnel or funding), which in turn results in changing priorities. Organizations might also experience changes in the ownership of third-party suppliers which could affect supply chain risk. Mission changes may require that organizations revisit underlying risk assumptions. For example, an organization whose mission is to collect threat information on possible domestic terrorist attacks and share such information with appropriate federal law enforcement and intelligence agencies may have its scope changed so that the organization is responsible for also sharing some of the information with local first responders. Such a change could affect assumptions regarding the security resources such users may have at their disposal. Changes in technology may also affect the underlying risk assumptions established by organizations. Unlike other types of change, technology changes may be totally independent of organizations, but still affect the risk organizations must address. For example, improvements in computing power may undermine assumptions regarding what constitutes sufficiently strong means of authentication (e.g., number of authentication factors) or cryptographic mechanism.

Automated Versus Manual Monitoring

Broadly speaking, organizations can conduct monitoring either by automated or manual methods. Where automated monitoring is feasible, it should be employed because it is generally faster, more efficient, and more cost-effective than manual monitoring. Automated monitoring is also less prone to human error. However, not all monitoring can take advantage of automation. Monitoring conducted at Tier 3 generally lends itself to automation where activities being monitored are information technology-based. Such activities can usually be detected, tracked, and monitored through the installation of appropriate software, hardware and/or firmware. To ensure that automated processes, procedures, and/or mechanisms supporting monitoring activities are providing the information needed, such processes, procedures, and mechanisms should be appropriately validated, updated and monitored. Compliance monitoring can be supported by automation when the risk mitigation measures being validated are information technology-based (e.g., installation of firewalls or testing of configuration settings on desktop computers). Such automated validation can often check whether risk mitigation measures are installed and whether the installations are correct. Similarly, effectiveness monitoring may also be supported by automation. If the threshold conditions for determining the effectiveness of risk response measures are predetermined, then automation can support such effectiveness monitoring. While automation can be a supporting capability for Tiers 1 and 2, generally automation does not provide substantive insight for non-information technology-based activities which are more prevalent at those higher tiers. Activities that are not as likely to benefit from automation include, for example, the use of multiple suppliers within the supply chain, evolving environments of operation, or evaluating the promise of emerging technical capabilities in support of missions/business functions. Where automated monitoring is not available, organizations employ manual monitoring and/or analysis.

Frequency of Monitoring

The frequency of risk monitoring (whether automated or manual) is driven by organizational missions/business functions and the ability of organizations to use the monitoring results to facilitate greater situational awareness. An increased level of situational awareness of the security state of organizational information systems and environments of operation helps organizations develop a better understanding of risk. Monitoring frequency is also driven by other factors, for example: (i) the anticipated frequency of changes in organizational information systems and operating environments; (ii) the potential impact of risk if not properly addressed through appropriate response measures; and (iii) the degree to which the threat space is changing. The frequency of monitoring can also be affected by the type of monitoring conducted (i.e., automated versus procedural approaches). Depending on the frequency of monitoring required by organizations, in most situations, monitoring is most efficient and cost-effective when automation is employed. Monitoring can provide significant benefits, especially in situations where such monitoring limits the opportunities for adversaries to gain a foothold within organizations (either through information systems or the environments in which those systems operate). When manual monitoring is employed by organizations, it is generally not efficient to perform the monitoring with the frequency that automation allows. In some instances, infrequent monitoring is not a major issue. For example, missions/business functions, facilities, legislation, policies, and technologies tend to change on a more gradual basis and as such, do not lend themselves to frequent monitoring. Instead, these types of changes are better suited to condition/event-based monitoring (e.g., if missions and/or business functions change, then monitoring of such changes is appropriate to determine if the changes have any impact on risk).

RISK MONITORING

TASK 4-2: Monitor organizational information systems and environments of operation on an ongoing basis to verify compliance, determine effectiveness of risk response measures, and identify changes.

Supplemental Guidance: Once organizations complete the development of their monitoring strategies, the strategies are implemented organization-wide. Because there are so many diverse aspects of monitoring, not all aspects of monitoring may be performed, or they may be performed at different times. The particular aspects of monitoring that are performed are dictated largely by the assumptions, constraints, risk tolerance, and priorities/trade-offs established by organizations during the risk framing step. For example, while organizations might desire to conduct all forms of monitoring (i.e., compliance, effectiveness, and change), the constraints imposed upon the organizations may allow only compliance monitoring that can be readily automated at Tier 3. If multiple aspects of monitoring can be supported, the output from the risk framing step helps organizations to determine the degree of emphasis and level of effort to place on the various monitoring activities.

As noted above, not all monitoring activities are conducted at the same tiers, for the same purpose, at the same time, or using the same techniques. However, it is important that organizations attempt to coordinate the various monitoring activities. Coordination of monitoring activities facilitates the sharing of risk-related information that may be useful for organizations in providing early warning, developing trend information, or allocating risk response measures in a timely and efficient manner. If monitoring is not coordinated, then the benefit of monitoring may be reduced, and could undermine the overall effort to identify and address risk. As feasible, organizations implement the various monitoring activities in a manner that maximizes the overall goal of monitoring, looking beyond the limited goals of particular monitoring activities. Risk monitoring results are applied in performing incremental risk assessments to maintain awareness of the risk being incurred, to highlight changes in risk, and to indicate the need to revisit other steps in the risk management process, as appropriate.

Outputs and Post Conditions

The output from the risk monitoring step is the information generated by: (i) verifying that required risk response measures are implemented and that information security requirements derived from and traceable to organizational missions/business functions, federal legislation, directives, regulations, policies, and standards/guidelines, are satisfied; (ii) determining the ongoing effectiveness of risk response measures; and (iii) identifying changes to organizational information systems and environments of operation. Outputs from the risk monitoring step can be useful inputs to the risk framing, risk assessment, and risk response steps. For example, compliance monitoring results may require that organizations revisit the implementation portion of the risk response step, while effectiveness monitoring results may require that organizations revisit the entire risk response step. The results of monitoring for changes to information systems and environments of operation may require organizations to revisit the risk assessment step. The results of the risk monitoring step can also serve the risk framing step (e.g., when organizations discover new threats or vulnerabilities that affect changes in organizational risk assumptions, risk tolerance, and/or priorities/trade-offs).

APPENDIX A

REFERENCES
LAWS, POLICIES, DIRECTIVES, INSTRUCTIONS, STANDARDS, AND GUIDELINES

LEGISLATION

1. E-Government Act [includes FISMA] (P.L. 107-347), December 2002.

2. Federal Information Security Management Act (P.L. 107-347, Title III), December 2002.

POLICIES, DIRECTIVES, INSTRUCTIONS

1. Committee on National Security Systems (CNSS) Instruction 4009, *National Information Assurance (IA) Glossary*, April 2010.

2. Committee on National Security Systems (CNSS) Instruction 1253, *Security Categorization and Control Selection for National Security Systems*, October 2009.

3. Office of Management and Budget, Circular A-130, Appendix III, Transmittal Memorandum #4, *Management of Federal Information Resources*, November 2000.

STANDARDS

1. National Institute of Standards and Technology Federal Information Processing Standards Publication 199, *Standards for Security Categorization of Federal Information and Information Systems*, February 2004.

2. National Institute of Standards and Technology Federal Information Processing Standards Publication 200, *Minimum Security Requirements for Federal Information and Information Systems*, March 2006.

3. ISO/IEC 15408:2005, *Common Criteria for Information Technology Security Evaluation*, 2005.

GUIDELINES

1. National Institute of Standards and Technology Special Publication 800-18, Revision 1, *Guide for Developing Security Plans for Federal Information Systems*, February 2006.

2. National Institute of Standards and Technology Special Publication 800-30, Revision 1, *Guide for Conducting Risk Assessments*, (Projected Publication Spring 2011).

3. National Institute of Standards and Technology Special Publication 800-37, Revision 1, *Guide for Applying the Risk Management Framework to Federal Information Systems: A Security Life Cycle Approach*, February 2010.

4. National Institute of Standards and Technology Special Publication 800-53, Revision 3, *Recommended Security Controls for Federal Information Systems and Organizations*, August 2009.

5. National Institute of Standards and Technology Special Publication 800-53A, Revision 1, *Guide for Assessing the Security Controls in Federal Information Systems and Organizations: Building Effective Security Assessment Plans*, June 2010.

6. National Institute of Standards and Technology Special Publication 800-59, *Guideline for Identifying an Information System as a National Security System*, August 2003.

7.   National Institute of Standards and Technology Special Publication 800-60, Revision 1, *Guide for Mapping Types of Information and Information Systems to Security Categories*, August 2008.

8.   National Institute of Standards and Technology Special Publication 800-70, Revision 1, *National Checklist Program for IT Products--Guidelines for Checklist Users and Developers*, September 2009.

9.   National Institute of Standards and Technology Special Publication 800-137, Initial Public Draft, *Information Security Continuous Monitoring for Federal Information Systems and Organizations*, December 2010.

APPENDIX B

GLOSSARY
COMMON TERMS AND DEFINITIONS

This appendix provides definitions for security terminology used within Special Publication 800-39. The terms in the glossary are consistent with the terms used in the suite of FISMA-related security standards and guidelines developed by NIST. Unless otherwise stated, all terms used in this publication are also consistent with the definitions contained in the CNSS Instruction 4009, *National Information Assurance (IA) Glossary.*

Adequate Security [OMB Circular A-130, Appendix III]	Security commensurate with the risk and magnitude of harm resulting from the loss, misuse, or unauthorized access to or modification of information.
Advanced Persistent Threat	An adversary that possesses sophisticated levels of expertise and significant resources which allow it to create opportunities to achieve its objectives by using multiple attack vectors (e.g., cyber, physical, and deception). These objectives typically include establishing and extending footholds within the information technology infrastructure of the targeted organizations for purposes of exfiltrating information, undermining or impeding critical aspects of a mission, program, or organization; or positioning itself to carry out these objectives in the future. The advanced persistent threat: (i) pursues its objectives repeatedly over an extended period of time; (ii) adapts to defenders' efforts to resist it; and (iii) is determined to maintain the level of interaction needed to execute its objectives.
Agency	See *Executive Agency.*
Assessment	See *Security Control Assessment.*
Assessor	See *Security Control Assessor.*
Assurance [CNSSI 4009]	Measure of confidence that the security features, practices, procedures, and architecture of an information system accurately mediates and enforces the security policy.
[NIST SP 800-53]	Grounds for confidence that the set of intended security controls in an information system are effective in their application.
Assurance Case [Software Engineering Institute, Carnegie Mellon University]	A structured set of arguments and a body of evidence showing that an information system satisfies specific claims with respect to a given quality attribute.
Authentication [FIPS 200]	Verifying the identity of a user, process, or device, often as a prerequisite to allowing access to resources in an information system.

Authenticity	The property of being genuine and being able to be verified and trusted; confidence in the validity of a transmission, a message, or message originator. See *Authentication*.
Authorization (to operate)	The official management decision given by a senior organizational official to authorize operation of an information system and to explicitly accept the risk to organizational operations (including mission, functions, image, or reputation), organizational assets, individuals, other organizations, and the Nation based on the implementation of an agreed-upon set of security controls.
Authorization Boundary [NIST SP 800-37]	All components of an information system to be authorized for operation by an authorizing official and excludes separately authorized systems, to which the information system is connected.
Authorizing Official [CNSSI 4009]	Senior (federal) official or executive with the authority to formally assume responsibility for operating an information system at an acceptable level of risk to organizational operations (including mission, functions, image, or reputation), organizational assets, individuals, other organizations, and the Nation.
Availability [44 U.S.C., Sec. 3542]	Ensuring timely and reliable access to and use of information.
Chief Information Officer [PL 104-106, Sec. 5125(b)]	Agency official responsible for: (i) Providing advice and other assistance to the head of the executive agency and other senior management personnel of the agency to ensure that information technology is acquired and information resources are managed in a manner that is consistent with laws, Executive Orders, directives, policies, regulations, and priorities established by the head of the agency; (ii) Developing, maintaining, and facilitating the implementation of a sound and integrated information technology architecture for the agency; and (iii) Promoting the effective and efficient design and operation of all major information resources management processes for the agency, including improvements to work processes of the agency.
Chief Information Security Officer	See *Senior Agency Information Security Officer*.
Classified National Security Information [CNSSI 4009]	Information that has been determined pursuant to Executive Order 13526 or any predecessor order to require protection against unauthorized disclosure and is marked to indicate its classified status when in documentary form.

Common Control
[NIST SP 800-37]

A security control that is inherited by one or more organizational information systems. See *Security Control Inheritance*.

Common Control Provider
[NIST SP 800-37]

An organizational official responsible for the development, implementation, assessment, and monitoring of common controls (i.e., security controls inherited by information systems).

Compensating Security Control
[CNSSI 4009]

A management, operational, and/or technical control (i.e., safeguard or countermeasure) employed by an organization in lieu of a recommended security control in the low, moderate, or high baselines that provides equivalent or comparable protection for an information system.

Confidentiality
[44 U.S.C., Sec. 3542]

Preserving authorized restrictions on information access and disclosure, including means for protecting personal privacy and proprietary information.

Course of Action (Risk Response)

A time-phased or situation-dependent combination of risk response measures.

Cyber Attack
[CNSSI 4009]

An attack, via cyberspace, targeting an enterprise's use of cyberspace for the purpose of disrupting, disabling, destroying, or maliciously controlling a computing environment/infrastructure; or destroying the integrity of the data or stealing controlled information.

Cyber Security
[CNSSI 4009]

The ability to protect or defend the use of cyberspace from cyber attacks.

Cyberspace
[CNSSI 4009]

A global domain within the information environment consisting of the interdependent network of information systems infrastructures including the Internet, telecommunications networks, computer systems, and embedded processors and controllers.

Defense-in-Breadth
[CNSSI 4009]

A planned, systematic set of multidisciplinary activities that seek to identify, manage, and reduce risk of exploitable vulnerabilities at every stage of the system, network, or subcomponent life cycle (system, network, or product design and development; manufacturing; packaging; assembly; system integration; distribution; operations; maintenance; and retirement).

Defense-in-Depth
[CNSSI 4009]

Information security strategy integrating people, technology, and operations capabilities to establish variable barriers across multiple layers and missions of the organization.

Enterprise [CNSSI 4009]	An organization with a defined mission/goal and a defined boundary, using information systems to execute that mission, and with responsibility for managing its own risks and performance. An enterprise may consist of all or some of the following business aspects: acquisition, program management, financial management (e.g., budgets), human resources, security, and information systems, information and mission management. See *Organization*.
Enterprise Architecture [CNSSI 4009]	The description of an enterprise's entire set of information systems: how they are configured, how they are integrated, how they interface to the external environment at the enterprise's boundary, how they are operated to support the enterprise mission, and how they contribute to the enterprise's overall security posture.
Environment of Operation [NIST SP 800-37]	The physical surroundings in which an information system processes, stores, and transmits information.
Executive Agency [41 U.S.C., Sec. 403]	An executive department specified in 5 U.S.C., Sec. 101; a military department specified in 5 U.S.C., Sec. 102; an independent establishment as defined in 5 U.S.C., Sec. 104(1); and a wholly owned Government corporation fully subject to the provisions of 31 U.S.C., Chapter 91.
Federal Agency	See *Executive Agency*.
Federal Information System [40 U.S.C., Sec. 11331]	An information system used or operated by an executive agency, by a contractor of an executive agency, or by another organization on behalf of an executive agency.
Hybrid Security Control [NIST SP 800-53]	A security control that is implemented in an information system in part as a common control and in part as a system-specific control. See *Common Control* and *System-Specific Security Control*.
Individuals	An assessment object that includes people applying specifications, mechanisms, or activities.
Industrial Control System	An information system used to control industrial processes such as manufacturing, product handling, production, and distribution. Industrial control systems include supervisory control and data acquisition systems used to control geographically dispersed assets, as well as distributed control systems and smaller control systems using programmable logic controllers to control localized processes.
Information [CNSSI 4009]	Any communication or representation of knowledge such as facts, data, or opinions in any medium or form, including textual, numerical, graphic, cartographic, narrative, or audiovisual.
[FIPS 199]	An instance of an information type.

Information Owner [CNSSI 4009]	Official with statutory or operational authority for specified information and responsibility for establishing the controls for its generation, classification, collection, processing, dissemination, and disposal. See *Information Steward*.
Information Resources [44 U.S.C., Sec. 3502]	Information and related resources, such as personnel, equipment, funds, and information technology.
Information Security [44 U.S.C., Sec. 3542]	The protection of information and information systems from unauthorized access, use, disclosure, disruption, modification, or destruction in order to provide confidentiality, integrity, and availability.
Information Security Architecture	An embedded, integral part of the enterprise architecture that describes the structure and behavior for an enterprise's security processes, information security systems, personnel and organizational sub-units, showing their alignment with the enterprise's mission and strategic plans.
Information Security Program Plan [NIST SP 800-53]	Formal document that provides an overview of the security requirements for an organization-wide information security program and describes the program management controls and common controls in place or planned for meeting those requirements.
Information Steward [CNSSI 4009]	An agency official with statutory or operational authority for specified information and responsibility for establishing the controls for its generation, collection, processing, dissemination, and disposal.
Information System [44 U.S.C., Sec. 3502]	A discrete set of information resources organized for the collection, processing, maintenance, use, sharing, dissemination, or disposition of information.
Information System Boundary	See *Authorization Boundary*.
Information System Owner (or Program Manager)	Official responsible for the overall procurement, development, integration, modification, or operation and maintenance of an information system.
Information System Resilience	The ability of an information system to continue to: (i) operate under adverse conditions or stress, even if in a degraded or debilitated state, while maintaining essential operational capabilities; and (ii) recover to an effective operational posture in a time frame consistent with mission needs.
Information System Security Officer	Individual assigned responsibility by the senior agency information security officer, authorizing official, management official, or information system owner for maintaining the appropriate operational security posture for an information system or program.

Information Security Risk

The risk to organizational operations (including mission, functions, image, reputation), organizational assets, individuals, other organizations, and the Nation due to the potential for unauthorized access, use, disclosure, disruption, modification, or destruction of information and/or information systems.

Information System-Related
Security Risks

Risks that arise through the loss of confidentiality, integrity, or availability of information or information systems and consider impacts to the organization (including assets, mission, functions, image, or reputation), individuals, other organizations, and the Nation. See *Risk*.

Information Technology
[40 U.S.C., Sec. 1401]

Any equipment or interconnected system or subsystem of equipment that is used in the automatic acquisition, storage, manipulation, management, movement, control, display, switching, interchange, transmission, or reception of data or information by the executive agency. For purposes of the preceding sentence, equipment is used by an executive agency if the equipment is used by the executive agency directly or is used by a contractor under a contract with the executive agency which: (i) requires the use of such equipment; or (ii) requires the use, to a significant extent, of such equipment in the performance of a service or the furnishing of a product. The term information technology includes computers, ancillary equipment, software, firmware, and similar procedures, services (including support services), and related resources.

Information Type
[FIPS 199]

A specific category of information (e.g., privacy, medical, proprietary, financial, investigative, contractor sensitive, security management) defined by an organization or in some instances, by a specific law, Executive Order, directive, policy, or regulation.

Integrity
[44 U.S.C., Sec. 3542]

Guarding against improper information modification or destruction, and includes ensuring information non-repudiation and authenticity.

Management Controls
[FIPS 200]

The security controls (i.e., safeguards or countermeasures) for an information system that focus on the management of risk and the management of information system security.

National Security System [44 U.S.C., Sec. 3542]	Any information system (including any telecommunications system) used or operated by an agency or by a contractor of an agency, or other organization on behalf of an agency (i) the function, operation, or use of which involves intelligence activities; involves cryptologic activities related to national security; involves command and control of military forces; involves equipment that is an integral part of a weapon or weapons system; or is critical to the direct fulfillment of military or intelligence missions (excluding a system that is to be used for routine administrative and business applications, for example, payroll, finance, logistics, and personnel management applications); or (ii) is protected at all times by procedures established for information that have been specifically authorized under criteria established by an Executive Order or an Act of Congress to be kept classified in the interest of national defense or foreign policy.
Operational Controls [FIPS 200]	The security controls (i.e., safeguards or countermeasures) for an information system that are primarily implemented and executed by people (as opposed to systems).
Organization [FIPS 200, Adapted]	An entity of any size, complexity, or positioning within an organizational structure (e.g., a federal agency or, as appropriate, any of its operational elements). See *Enterprise*.
Plan of Action and Milestones [OMB Memorandum 02-01]	A document that identifies tasks needing to be accomplished. It details resources required to accomplish the elements of the plan, any milestones in meeting the tasks, and scheduled completion dates for the milestones.
Reciprocity	Mutual agreement among participating organizations to accept each other's security assessments in order to reuse information system resources and/or to accept each other's assessed security posture in order to share information.
Resilience	See *Information System Resilience*.
Risk [CNSSI 4009]	A measure of the extent to which an entity is threatened by a potential circumstance or event, and typically a function of: (i) the adverse impacts that would arise if the circumstance or event occurs; and (ii) the likelihood of occurrence. [Note: Information system-related security risks are those risks that arise from the loss of confidentiality, integrity, or availability of information or information systems and reflect the potential adverse impacts to organizational operations (including mission, functions, image, or reputation), organizational assets, individuals, other organizations, and the Nation.]

Risk Assessment	The process of identifying risks to organizational operations (including mission, functions, image, reputation), organizational assets, individuals, other organizations, and the Nation, resulting from the operation of an information system.

Part of risk management, incorporates threat and vulnerability analyses, and considers mitigations provided by security controls planned or in place. Synonymous with risk analysis. |
Risk Executive (Function) [CNSSI 4009]	An individual or group within an organization that helps to ensure that: (i) security risk-related considerations for individual information systems, to include the authorization decisions for those systems, are viewed from an organization-wide perspective with regard to the overall strategic goals and objectives of the organization in carrying out its missions and business functions; and (ii) managing risk from individual information systems is consistent across the organization, reflects organizational risk tolerance, and is considered along with other organizational risks affecting mission/business success.
Risk Management [CNSSI 4009, adapted]	The program and supporting processes to manage information security risk to organizational operations (including mission, functions, image, reputation), organizational assets, individuals, other organizations, and the Nation, and includes: (i) establishing the context for risk-related activities; (ii) assessing risk; (iii) responding to risk once determined; and (iv) monitoring risk over time.
Risk Mitigation [CNSSI 4009]	Prioritizing, evaluating, and implementing the appropriate risk-reducing controls/countermeasures recommended from the risk management process.
Risk Monitoring	Maintaining ongoing awareness of an organization's risk environment, risk management program, and associated activities to support risk decisions.
Risk Response	Accepting, avoiding, mitigating, sharing, or transferring risk to organizational operations (i.e., mission, functions, image, or reputation), organizational assets, individuals, other organizations, or the Nation.
Risk Response Measure	A specific action taken to respond to an identified risk.
Root Cause Analysis	A principle-based, systems approach for the identification of underlying causes associated with a particular set of risks.
Security Authorization (to Operate)	See *Authorization (to operate)*.

Security Categorization	The process of determining the security category for information or an information system. Security categorization methodologies are described in CNSS Instruction 1253 for national security systems and in FIPS 199 for other than national security systems.
Security Control Assessment [CNSSI 4009, Adapted]	The testing and/or evaluation of the management, operational, and technical security controls to determine the extent to which the controls are implemented correctly, operating as intended, and producing the desired outcome with respect to meeting the security requirements for an information system or organization.
Security Control Assessor	The individual, group, or organization responsible for conducting a security control assessment.
Security Control Baseline [CNSSI 4009]	The set of minimum security controls defined for a low-impact, moderate-impact, or high-impact information system.
Security Control Enhancements	Statements of security capability to: (i) build in additional, but related, functionality to a basic control; and/or (ii) increase the strength of a basic control.
Security Control Inheritance [CNSSI 4009]	A situation in which an information system or application receives protection from security controls (or portions of security controls) that are developed, implemented, assessed, authorized, and monitored by entities other than those responsible for the system or application; entities either internal or external to the organization where the system or application resides. See *Common Control*.
Security Controls [FIPS 199, CNSSI 4009]	The management, operational, and technical controls (i.e., safeguards or countermeasures) prescribed for an information system to protect the confidentiality, integrity, and availability of the system and its information.
Security Impact Analysis [NIST SP 800-37]	The analysis conducted by an organizational official to determine the extent to which changes to the information system have affected the security state of the system.
Security Objective [FIPS 199]	Confidentiality, integrity, or availability.
Security Plan [NIST SP 800-18]	Formal document that provides an overview of the security requirements for an information system or an information security program and describes the security controls in place or planned for meeting those requirements. See *System Security Plan* or *Information Security Program Plan*.
Security Policy [CNSSI 4009]	A set of criteria for the provision of security services.

Security Requirements [FIPS 200]	Requirements levied on an information system that are derived from applicable laws, Executive Orders, directives, policies, standards, instructions, regulations, procedures, or organizational mission/business case needs to ensure the confidentiality, integrity, and availability of the information being processed, stored, or transmitted.
Senior Agency Information Security Officer [44 U.S.C., Sec. 3544]	Official responsible for carrying out the Chief Information Officer responsibilities under FISMA and serving as the Chief Information Officer's primary liaison to the agency's authorizing officials, information system owners, and information system security officers. [Note: Organizations subordinate to federal agencies may use the term *Senior Information Security Officer* or *Chief Information Security Officer* to denote individuals filling positions with similar responsibilities to Senior Agency Information Security Officers.]
Senior Information Security Officer	See *Senior Agency Information Security Officer*.
Subsystem	A major subdivision or component of an information system consisting of information, information technology, and personnel that performs one or more specific functions.
Supplementation (Security Controls)	The process of adding security controls or control enhancements to a security control baseline from NIST Special Publication 800-53 or CNSS Instruction 1253 in order to adequately meet the organization's risk management needs.
System	See *Information System*.
System Security Plan [NIST SP 800-18]	Formal document that provides an overview of the security requirements for an information system and describes the security controls in place or planned for meeting those requirements.
System-Specific Security Control [NIST SP 800-37]	A security control for an information system that has not been designated as a common control or the portion of a hybrid control that is to be implemented within an information system.
Tailoring [NIST SP 800-53, CNSSI 4009]	The process by which a security control baseline is modified based on: (i) the application of scoping guidance; (ii) the specification of compensating security controls, if needed; and (iii) the specification of organization-defined parameters in the security controls via explicit assignment and selection statements.
Tailored Security Control Baseline	A set of security controls resulting from the application of tailoring guidance to the security control baseline. See *Tailoring*.

Technical Controls [FIPS 200]	Security controls (i.e., safeguards or countermeasures) for an information system that are primarily implemented and executed by the information system through mechanisms contained in the hardware, software, or firmware components of the system.
Threat [CNSSI 4009]	Any circumstance or event with the potential to adversely impact organizational operations (including mission, functions, image, or reputation), organizational assets, individuals, other organizations, or the Nation through an information system via unauthorized access, destruction, disclosure, modification of information, and/or denial of service.
Threat Assessment [CNSSI 4009]	Process of formally evaluating the degree of threat to an information system or enterprise and describing the nature of the threat.
Threat Source [CNSSI 4009]	The intent and method targeted at the intentional exploitation of a vulnerability or a situation and method that may accidentally exploit a vulnerability.
Trustworthiness [CNSSI 4009]	The attribute of a person or enterprise that provides confidence to others of the qualifications, capabilities, and reliability of that entity to perform specific tasks and fulfill assigned responsibilities.
Vulnerability [CNSSI 4009]	Weakness in an information system, system security procedures, internal controls, or implementation that could be exploited by a threat source.
Vulnerability Assessment [CNSSI 4009]	Systematic examination of an information system or product to determine the adequacy of security measures, identify security deficiencies, provide data from which to predict the effectiveness of proposed security measures, and confirm the adequacy of such measures after implementation.

APPENDIX C

ACRONYMS

COMMON ABBREVIATIONS

APT	Advanced Persistent Threat
CIO	Chief Information Officer
CNSS	Committee on National Security Systems
COTS	Commercial Off-The-Shelf
DoD	Department of Defense
FIPS	Federal Information Processing Standards
FISMA	Federal Information Security Management Act
IA	Information Assurance
ICS	Industrial Control System
IEC	International Electrotechnical Commission
ISO	International Organization for Standardization
NIST	National Institute of Standards and Technology
NSA	National Security Agency
ODNI	Office of the Director of National Intelligence
OMB	Office of Management and Budget
POAM	Plan of Action and Milestones
RMF	Risk Management Framework
SCAP	Security Content Automation Protocol
SP	Special Publication
U.S.C.	United States Code

APPENDIX D

ROLES AND RESPONSIBILITIES
KEY PARTICIPANTS IN THE RISK MANAGEMENT PROCESS

The following sections describe the roles and responsibilities[66] of key participants involved in an organization's risk management process.[67] Recognizing that organizations have widely varying missions and organizational structures, there may be differences in naming conventions for risk management-related roles and how specific responsibilities are allocated among organizational personnel (e.g., multiple individuals filling a single role or one individual filling multiple roles).[68] However, the basic functions remain the same. The application of the risk management process across the three risk management tiers described in this publication is flexible, allowing organizations to effectively accomplish the intent of the specific tasks within their respective organizational structures to best manage risk.

D.1 HEAD OF AGENCY (CHIEF EXECUTIVE OFFICER)

The *head of agency* (or chief executive officer) is the highest-level senior official or executive within an organization with the overall responsibility to provide information security protections commensurate with the risk and magnitude of harm (i.e., impact) to organizational operations and assets, individuals, other organizations, and the Nation resulting from unauthorized access, use, disclosure, disruption, modification, or destruction of: (i) information collected or maintained by or on behalf of the agency; and (ii) information systems used or operated by an agency or by a contractor of an agency or other organization on behalf of an agency. Agency heads are also responsible for ensuring that: (i) information security management processes are integrated with strategic and operational planning processes; (ii) senior officials within the organization provide information security for the information and information systems that support the operations and assets under their control; and (iii) the organization has trained personnel sufficient to assist in complying with the information security requirements in related legislation, policies, directives, instructions, standards, and guidelines. Through the development and implementation of strong policies, the head of agency establishes the organizational commitment to information security and the actions required to effectively manage risk and protect the missions/business functions being carried out by the organization. The head of agency establishes appropriate accountability for information security and provides active support and oversight of monitoring and improvement for the information security program. Senior leadership commitment to information security establishes a level of due diligence within the organization that promotes a climate for mission and business success.

D.2 RISK EXECUTIVE (FUNCTION)

The *risk executive (function)* is an individual or group within an organization that provides a more comprehensive, organization-wide approach to risk management. The risk executive (function) serves as the common risk management resource for senior leaders/executives, mission/business

---

[66] The roles and responsibilities described in this appendix are consistent with the roles and responsibilities associated with the Risk Management Framework in NIST Special Publication 800-37.

[67] Organizations may define other roles (e.g., facilities manager, human resources manager, systems administrator) to support the risk management process.

[68] Caution is exercised when one individual fills multiples roles in the risk management process to ensure that the individual retains an appropriate level of independence and remains free from conflicts of interest.

owners, chief information officers, chief information security officers, information system owners, common control providers, enterprise architects, information security architects, information systems/security engineers, information system security managers/officers, and any other stakeholders having a vested interest in the mission/business success of organizations. The risk executive (function) coordinates with senior leaders/executives to:

- Establish risk management roles and responsibilities;

- Develop and implement an organization-wide *risk management strategy* that guides and informs organizational risk decisions (including how risk is framed, assessed, responded to, and monitored over time);

- Manage threat and vulnerability information with regard to organizational information systems and the environments in which the systems operate;

- Establish organization-wide forums to consider all types and sources of risk (including aggregated risk);

- Determine organizational risk based on the aggregated risk from the operation and use of information systems and the respective environments of operation;

- Provide oversight for the risk management activities carried out by organizations to ensure consistent and effective risk-based decisions;

- Develop a greater understanding of risk with regard to the strategic view of organizations and their integrated operations;

- Establish effective vehicles and serve as a focal point for communicating and sharing risk-related information among key stakeholders internally and externally to organizations;

- Specify the degree of autonomy for subordinate organizations permitted by parent organizations with regard to framing, assessing, responding to, and monitoring risk;

- Promote cooperation and collaboration among authorizing officials to include security authorization actions requiring shared responsibility (e.g., joint/leveraged authorizations);

- Ensure that security authorization decisions consider all factors necessary for mission and business success; and

- Ensure shared responsibility for supporting organizational missions and business functions using external providers receives the needed visibility and is elevated to appropriate decision-making authorities.

The risk executive (function) presumes neither a specific organizational structure nor formal responsibility assigned to any one individual or group within the organization. Heads of agencies or organizations may choose to retain the risk executive (function) or to delegate the function. The risk executive (function) requires a mix of skills, expertise, and perspectives to understand the strategic goals and objectives of organizations, organizational missions/business functions, technical possibilities and constraints, and key mandates and guidance that shape organizational operations. To provide this needed mixture, the risk executive (function) can be filled by a single individual or office (supported by an expert staff) or by a designated group (e.g., a risk board, executive steering committee, executive leadership council). The risk executive (function) fits into the organizational governance structure in such a way as to facilitate efficiency and effectiveness.

D.3 CHIEF INFORMATION OFFICER

The *chief information officer*[69] is an organizational official responsible for: (i) designating a senior information security officer; (ii) developing and maintaining information security policies, procedures, and control techniques to address all applicable requirements; (iii) overseeing personnel with significant responsibilities for information security and ensuring that the personnel are adequately trained; (iv) assisting senior organizational officials concerning their security responsibilities; and (v) in coordination with other senior officials, reporting annually to the head of the federal agency on the overall effectiveness of the organization's information security program, including progress of remedial actions. The chief information officer, with the support of the risk executive (function) and the senior information security officer, works closely with authorizing officials and their designated representatives to help ensure that:

- An organization-wide information security program is effectively implemented resulting in adequate security for all organizational information systems and environments of operation for those systems;

- Information security considerations are integrated into programming/planning/budgeting cycles, enterprise architectures, and acquisition/system development life cycles;

- Information systems are covered by approved security plans and are authorized to operate;

- Information security-related activities required across the organization are accomplished in an efficient, cost-effective, and timely manner; and

- There is centralized reporting of appropriate information security-related activities.

The chief information officer and authorizing officials also determine, based on organizational priorities, the appropriate allocation of resources dedicated to the protection of the information systems supporting the organization's missions and business functions. For selected information systems, the chief information officer may be designated as an authorizing official or a co-authorizing official with other senior organizational officials. The role of chief information officer has inherent U.S. Government authority and is assigned to government personnel only.

D.4 INFORMATION OWNER/STEWARD

The *information owner/steward* is an organizational official with statutory, management, or operational authority for specified information and the responsibility for establishing the policies and procedures governing its generation, collection, processing, dissemination, and disposal.[70] In information-sharing environments, the information owner/steward is responsible for establishing the rules for appropriate use and protection of the subject information (e.g., rules of behavior) and retains that responsibility when the information is shared with or provided to other organizations. The owner/steward of the information processed, stored, or transmitted by an information system

---

[69] When an organization has not designated a formal chief information officer position, FISMA requires the associated responsibilities to be handled by a comparable organizational official.

[70] Federal information is an asset of the Nation, not of a particular federal agency or its subordinate organizations. In that spirit, many federal agencies are developing policies, procedures, processes, and training needed to end the practice of *information ownership* and implement the practice of *information stewardship*. Information stewardship is the careful and responsible management of federal information belonging to the Nation as a whole, regardless of the entity or source that may have originated, created, or compiled the information. Information stewards provide maximum access to federal information to elements of the federal government and its customers, balanced by the obligation to protect the information in accordance with the provisions of FISMA and any associated security-related federal policies, directives, regulations, standards, and guidance.

may or may not be the same as the system owner. A single information system may contain information from multiple information owners/stewards. Information owners/stewards provide input to information system owners regarding the security requirements and security controls for the systems where the information is processed, stored, or transmitted.

D.5 SENIOR INFORMATION SECURITY OFFICER

The *senior information security officer* is an organizational official responsible for: (i) carrying out the chief information officer security responsibilities under FISMA; and (ii) serving as the primary liaison for the chief information officer to the organization's authorizing officials, information system owners, common control providers, and information system security officers. The senior information security officer: (i) possesses professional qualifications, including training and experience, required to administer the information security program functions; (ii) maintains information security duties as a primary responsibility; and (iii) heads an office with the mission and resources to assist the organization in achieving more secure information and information systems in accordance with the requirements in FISMA. The senior information security officer (or supporting staff members) may also serve as authorizing official designated representatives or security control assessors. The role of senior information security officer has inherent U.S. Government authority and is assigned to government personnel only.

D.6 AUTHORIZING OFFICIAL

The *authorizing official* is a senior official or executive with the authority to formally assume responsibility for operating an information system at an acceptable level of risk to organizational operations and assets, individuals, other organizations, and the Nation.[71] Authorizing officials typically have budgetary oversight for an information system *or* are responsible for the mission and/or business operations supported by the system. Through the security authorization process, authorizing officials are *accountable* for the security risks associated with information system operations. Accordingly, authorizing officials are in management positions with a level of authority commensurate with understanding and accepting such information system-related security risks. Authorizing officials also approve security plans, memorandums of agreement or understanding, and plans of action and milestones and determine whether significant changes in the information systems or environments of operation require reauthorization. Authorizing officials can deny authorization to operate an information system or if the system is operational, halt operations, if unacceptable risks exist. Authorizing officials coordinate their activities with the risk executive (function), chief information officer, senior information security officer, common control providers, information system owners, information system security officers, security control assessors, and other interested parties during the security authorization process. With the increasing complexity of mission/business processes, partnership arrangements, and the use of external/shared services, it is possible that a particular information system may involve multiple authorizing officials. If so, agreements are established among the authorizing officials and documented in the security plan. Authorizing officials are responsible for ensuring that all activities and functions associated with security authorization that are delegated to authorizing official designated representatives are carried out. The role of authorizing official has inherent U.S. Government authority and is assigned to government personnel only.

---

[71] The responsibility of authorizing officials described in FIPS 200, was extended in NIST Special Publication 800-53 to include risks to other organizations and the Nation.

D.7 AUTHORIZING OFFICIAL DESIGNATED REPRESENTATIVE

The *authorizing official designated representative* is an organizational official that acts on behalf of an authorizing official to coordinate and conduct the required day-to-day activities associated with the security authorization process. Authorizing official designated representatives can be empowered by authorizing officials to make certain decisions with regard to the planning and resourcing of the security authorization process, approval of the security plan, approval and monitoring the implementation of plans of action and milestones, and the assessment and/or determination of risk. The designated representative may also be called upon to prepare the final authorization package, obtain the authorizing official's signature on the authorization decision document, and transmit the authorization package to appropriate organizational officials. The only activity that cannot be delegated to the designated representative by the authorizing official is the authorization decision and signing of the associated authorization decision document (i.e., the acceptance of risk to organizational operations and assets, individuals, other organizations, and the Nation).

D.8 COMMON CONTROL PROVIDER

The *common control provider* is an individual, group, or organization responsible for the development, implementation, assessment, and monitoring of common controls (i.e., security controls inherited by information systems).[72] Common control providers are responsible for: (i) documenting the organization-identified common controls in a *security plan* (or equivalent document prescribed by the organization); (ii) ensuring that required assessments of common controls are carried out by qualified assessors with an appropriate level of independence defined by the organization; (iii) documenting assessment findings in a *security assessment report*; and (iv) producing a *plan of action and milestones* for all controls having weaknesses or deficiencies. Security plans, security assessment reports, and plans of action and milestones for common controls (or a summary of such information) is made available to information system owners *inheriting* those controls after the information is reviewed and approved by the senior official or executive with oversight responsibility for those controls.

D.9 INFORMATION SYSTEM OWNER

The *information system owner* is an organizational official responsible for the procurement, development, integration, modification, operation, maintenance, and disposal of an information system.[73] The information system owner is responsible for addressing the operational interests of the user community (i.e., individuals who depend upon the information system to satisfy mission, business, or operational requirements) and for ensuring compliance with information security requirements. In coordination with the information system security officer, the information system owner is responsible for the development and maintenance of the security plan and ensures that the system is deployed and operated in accordance with the agreed-upon security controls. In coordination with the information owner/steward, the information system owner is

---

[72] Organizations can have multiple common control providers depending on how information security responsibilities are allocated organization-wide. Common control providers may also be *information system owners* when the common controls are resident within an information system.

[73] The *information system owner* serves as the focal point for the information system. In that capacity, the information system owner serves both as an owner and as the central point of contact between the authorization process and the owners of components of the system including, for example: (i) applications, networking, servers, or workstations; (ii) owners/stewards of information processed, stored, or transmitted by the system; and (iii) owners of the missions and business functions supported by the system. Some organizations may refer to information system owners as program managers or business/asset owners.

also responsible for deciding who has access to the system (and with what types of privileges or access rights)[74] and ensures that system users and support personnel receive the requisite security training (e.g., instruction in rules of behavior). Based on guidance from the authorizing official, the information system owner informs appropriate organizational officials of the need to conduct the security authorization, ensures that the necessary resources are available for the effort, and provides the required information system access, information, and documentation to the security control assessor. The information system owner receives the security assessment results from the security control assessor. After taking appropriate steps to reduce or eliminate vulnerabilities, the information system owner assembles the authorization package and submits the package to the authorizing official or the authorizing official designated representative for adjudication.[75]

D.10 INFORMATION SYSTEM SECURITY OFFICER

The *information system security officer*[76] is an individual responsible for ensuring that the appropriate operational security posture is maintained for an information system and as such, works in close collaboration with the information system owner. The information system security officer also serves as a principal advisor on all matters, technical and otherwise, involving the security of an information system. The information system security officer has the detailed knowledge and expertise required to manage the security aspects of an information system and, in many organizations, is assigned responsibility for the day-to-day security operations of a system. This responsibility may also include, but is not limited to, physical and environmental protection, personnel security, incident handling, and security training and awareness. The information system security officer may be called upon to assist in the development of the security policies and procedures and to ensure compliance with those policies and procedures. In close coordination with the information system owner, the information system security officer often plays an active role in the monitoring of a system and its environment of operation to include developing and updating the security plan, managing and controlling changes to the system, and assessing the security impact of those changes.

D.11 INFORMATION SECURITY ARCHITECT

The *information security architect* is an individual, group, or organization responsible for ensuring that the information security requirements necessary to protect the organizational missions/business functions are adequately addressed in all aspects of enterprise architecture including reference models, segment and solution architectures, and the resulting information systems supporting those missions and business processes. The information security architect serves as the liaison between the enterprise architect and the information system security engineer and also coordinates with information system owners, common control providers, and information system security officers on the allocation of security controls as system-specific, hybrid, or common controls. In addition, information security architects, in close coordination with information system security officers, advise authorizing officials, chief information officers,

---

[74] The responsibility for deciding who has access to specific information within an information system (and with what types of privileges or access rights) may reside with the information owner/steward.

[75] Depending on how the organization has organized its security authorization activities, the authorizing official may choose to designate an individual other than the information system owner to compile and assemble the information for the security authorization package. In this situation, the designated individual must coordinate the compilation and assembly activities with the information system owner.

[76] Organizations may also define an *information system security manager* or *information security manager* role with similar responsibilities as an information system security officer or with oversight responsibilities for an information security program. In these situations, information system security officers may, at the discretion of the organization, report directly to information system security managers or information security managers.

senior information security officers, and the risk executive (function), on a range of security-related issues including, for example, establishing information system boundaries, assessing the severity of weaknesses and deficiencies in the information system, plans of action and milestones, risk mitigation approaches, security alerts, and potential adverse effects of vulnerabilities.

D.12 INFORMATION SYSTEM SECURITY ENGINEER

The *information system security engineer* is an individual, group, or organization responsible for conducting information system security engineering activities. Information system security engineering is a process that captures and refines information security requirements and ensures that the requirements are effectively integrated into information technology component products and information systems through purposeful security architecting, design, development, and configuration. Information system security engineers are an integral part of the development team (e.g., integrated project team) designing and developing organizational information systems or upgrading legacy systems. Information system security engineers employ best practices when implementing security controls within an information system including software engineering methodologies, system/security engineering principles, secure design, secure architecture, and secure coding techniques. System security engineers coordinate their security-related activities with information security architects, senior information security officers, information system owners, common control providers, and information system security officers.

D.13 SECURITY CONTROL ASSESSOR

The *security control assessor* is an individual, group, or organization responsible for conducting a comprehensive assessment of the management, operational, and technical security controls employed within or inherited by an information system to determine the overall effectiveness of the controls (i.e., the extent to which the controls are implemented correctly, operating as intended, and producing the desired outcome with respect to meeting the security requirements for the system). Security control assessors also provide an assessment of the severity of weaknesses or deficiencies discovered in the information system and its environment of operation and recommend corrective actions to address identified vulnerabilities. In addition to the above responsibilities, security control assessors prepare the final security assessment report containing the results and findings from the assessment. Prior to initiating the security control assessment, an assessor conducts an assessment of the security plan to help ensure that the plan provides a set of security controls for the information system that meet the stated security requirements.

The required level of assessor independence is determined by the specific conditions of the security control assessment. For example, when the assessment is conducted in support of an authorization decision or ongoing authorization, the authorizing official makes an explicit determination of the degree of independence required in accordance with federal policies, directives, standards, and guidelines. Assessor independence is an important factor in: (i) preserving the impartial and unbiased nature of the assessment process; (ii) determining the credibility of the security assessment results; and (iii) ensuring that the authorizing official receives the most objective information possible in order to make an informed, risk-based, authorization decision. The information system owner and common control provider rely on the security expertise and the technical judgment of the assessor to: (i) assess the security controls employed within and inherited by the information system using assessment procedures specified in the security assessment plan; and (ii) provide specific recommendations on how to correct weaknesses or deficiencies in the controls and address identified vulnerabilities.

APPENDIX E

RISK MANAGEMENT PROCESS TASKS

SUMMARY OF TASKS FOR STEPS IN THE RISK MANAGEMENT PROCESS

TASK	TASK DESCRIPTION
Step 1: Risk Framing	
TASK 1-1 RISK ASSUMPTIONS	Identify assumptions that affect how risk is assessed, responded to, and monitored within the organization.
TASK 1-2 RISK CONSTRAINTS	Identify constraints on the conduct of risk assessment, risk response, and risk monitoring activities within the organization.
TASK 1-3 RISK TOLERANCE	Identify the level of risk tolerance for the organization.
TASK 1-4 PRIORITIES AND TRADE-OFFS	Identify priorities and trade-offs considered by the organization in managing risk.
Step 2: Risk Assessment	
TASK 2-1 THREAT AND VULNERABILITY IDENTIFICATION	Identify threats to and vulnerabilities in organizational information systems and the environments in which the systems operate.
TASK 2-2 RISK DETERMINATION	Determine the risk to organizational operations and assets, individuals, other organizations, and the Nation if identified threats exploit identified vulnerabilities.
Step 3: Risk Response	
TASK 3-1 RISK RESPONSE IDENTIFICATION	Identify alternative courses of action to respond to risk determined during the risk assessment.
TASK 3-2 EVALUATION OF ALTERNATIVES	Evaluate alternative courses of action for responding to risk.
TASK 3-3 RISK RESPONSE DECISION	Decide on the appropriate course of action for responding to risk.
TASK 3-4 RISK RESPONSE IMPLEMENTATION	Implement the course of action selected to respond to risk.
Step 4: Risk Monitoring	
TASK 4-1 RISK MONITORING STRATEGY	Develop a risk monitoring strategy for the organization that includes the purpose, type, and frequency of monitoring activities.
TASK 4-2 RISK MONITORING	Monitor organizational information systems and environments of operation on an ongoing basis to verify compliance, determine effectiveness of risk response measures, and identify changes.

APPENDIX F

GOVERNANCE MODELS

APPROACHES TO INFORMATION SECURITY GOVERNANCE

Three approaches to information security governance can be used to meet organizational needs: (i) a *centralized* approach; (ii) a *decentralized* approach; or (iii) a *hybrid* approach. The authority, responsibility, and decision-making power related to information security and risk management differ in each governance approach. The appropriate governance structure for an organization varies based on many factors (e.g., mission/business needs; culture and size of the organization; geographic distribution of organizational operations, assets, and individuals; and risk tolerance). The information security governance structure is aligned with other governance structures (e.g., information technology governance) to ensure compatibility with the established management practices within the organization and to increase its overall effectiveness.

Centralized Governance

In centralized governance structures, the authority, responsibility, and decision-making power are vested solely within central bodies. These centralized bodies establish the appropriate policies, procedures, and processes for ensuring organization-wide involvement in the development and implementation of risk management and information security strategies, risk, and information security decisions, and the creation inter-organizational and intra-organizational communication mechanisms. A centralized approach to governance requires strong, well-informed central leadership and provides consistency throughout the organization. Centralized governance structures also provide less autonomy for subordinate organizations that are part of the parent organization.

Decentralized Governance

In decentralized information security governance structures, the authority, responsibility, and decision-making power are vested in and delegated to individual subordinate organizations within the parent organization (e.g., bureaus/components within an executive department of the federal government or business units within a corporation). Subordinate organizations establish their own policies, procedures, and processes for ensuring (sub) organization-wide involvement in the development and implementation of risk management and information security strategies, risk and information security decisions, and the creation of mechanisms to communicate within the organization. A decentralized approach to information security governance accommodates subordinate organizations with divergent mission/business needs and operating environments at the cost of consistency throughout the organization as a whole. The effectiveness of this approach is greatly increased by the sharing of risk-related information among subordinate organizations so that no subordinate organization is able to transfer risk to another without the latter's informed consent. It is also important to share risk-related information with parent organizations as the risk decisions by subordinate organizations may have an effect on the organization as a whole.

Hybrid Governance

In hybrid information security governance structures, the authority, responsibility, and decision-making power are distributed between a central body and individual subordinate organizations. The central body establishes the policies, procedures, and processes for ensuring organization-wide involvement in the portion of the risk management and information security strategies and decisions affecting the entire organization (e.g., decisions related to shared infrastructure or common security services). Subordinate organizations, in a similar manner, establish appropriate policies, procedures, and processes for ensuring their involvement in the portion of the risk management and information security strategies and decisions that are specific to their mission/business needs and environments of operation. A hybrid approach to governance requires strong, well-informed leadership for the organization as a whole and for subordinate organizations, and provides consistency throughout the organization for those aspects of risk and information security that affect the entire organization.

APPENDIX G

TRUST MODELS

APPROACHES TO ESTABLISHING TRUST RELATIONSIPS

The following trust models describe ways in which organizations can obtain the levels of trust needed to form partnerships, collaborate with other organizations, share information, or receive information system/security services. No single trust model is inherently better than any other model. Rather, each model provides organizations with certain advantages and disadvantages based on their circumstances (e.g., governance structure, risk tolerance, and criticality/sensitivity of organizational missions and business processes).

Validated Trust

In the *validated trust model*, one organization obtains a body of evidence regarding the actions of another organization (e.g., the organization's information security policies, activities, and risk-related decisions) and uses that evidence to establish a level of trust with the other organization. An example of validated trust is where one organization develops an application or information system and provides evidence (e.g., security plan, assessment results) to a second organization that supports the claims by the first organization that the application/system meets certain security requirements and/or addresses the appropriate security controls in NIST Special Publication 800-53. Validated trust may not be sufficient—that is, the evidence offered by the first organization to the second organization may not fully satisfy the second organization's trust requirements or trust expectations. The more evidence provided between organizations as well as the quality of such evidence, the greater the degree of trust that can be achieved. Trust is linked to the degree of transparency between the two organizations with regard to risk and information security-related activities and decisions.

Direct Historical Trust

In the *direct historical trust model*, the track record exhibited by an organization in the past, particularly in its risk and information security-related activities and decisions, can contribute to and help establish a level of trust with other organizations. While validated trust models assume that an organization provides the required level of evidence needed to establish trust, obtaining such evidence may not always be possible. In such instances, trust may be based on other deciding factors, including the organization's historical relationship with the other organization or its recent experience in working with the other organization. For example, if one organization has worked with a second organization for years doing some activity and has not had any negative experiences, the first organization may be willing to trust the second organization in working on another activity, even though the organizations do not share any common experience for that particular activity. Direct historical trust tends to build up over time with the more positive experiences contributing to increased levels of trust between organizations. Conversely, negative experiences may cause trust levels to decrease among organizations.

Mediated Trust

In the *mediated trust model*, an organization establishes a level of trust with another organization based on assurances provided by some mutually trusted third party. There are several types of mediated trust models that can be employed. For example, two organizations attempting to establish a trust relationship may not have a direct trust history between the two organizations, but do have a trust relationship with a third organization. The third party that is trusted by both organizations, brokers the trust relationship between the two organizations, thus helping to establish the required level of trust. Another type of mediated trust involves the concept of transitivity of trust. In this example, one organization establishes a trust relationship with a second organization. Independent of the first trust relationship, the second organization establishes a trust relationship with a third organization. Since the first organization trusts the second organization and the second organization trusts the third organization, a trust relationship is now established between the first and third organizations (illustrating the concept of transitive trust among organizations).[77]

Mandated Trust

In the *mandated trust model*, an organization establishes a level of trust with another organization based on a specific mandate issued by a third party in a position of authority.[78] This mandate can be established by the respective authority through Executive Orders, directives, regulations, or policies (e.g., a memorandum from an agency head directing that all subordinate organizations accept the results of security assessments conducted by any subordinate organization within the agency). Mandated trust can also be established when some organizational entity is decreed to be the authoritative source for the provision of information resources including information technology products, systems, or services. For example, an organization may be given the responsibility and the authority to issue Public Key Infrastructure (PKI) certificates for a group of organizations.

Hybrid Trust

In general, the trust models described above are not mutually exclusive. Each of the trust models may be used independently as a stand-alone model or in conjunction with another model. Several trust models may be used at times within the organization (e.g., at various phases in the system development life cycle). Also, since organizations are often large and diverse, it is possible that subordinate organizations within a parent organization might independently employ different trust models in establishing trust relationships with potential partnering organizations (including subordinate organizations). The organizational governance structure may establish the specific terms and conditions for how the various trust models are employed in a complementary manner within the organization.

Suitability of Various Trust Models

The trust models can be employed at various tiers in the risk management approach described in this publication. None of the trust models is inherently better or worse than the others. However, some models may be better suited to some situations than others. For example, the validated trust model, because it requires evidence of a technical nature (e.g., tests completed successfully), is probably best suited for application at Tier 3. In contrast, the direct historical trust model, with a significant emphasis on past experiences, is more suited for application at Tiers 1 or 2. The mediated and mandated trust models are typically more oriented toward governance and consequently are best suited for application at Tier 1. However, some implementations of the mandated trust model, for example, being required to trust the source of a PKI certificate, are more oriented toward Tier 3. Similarly, although the mediated trust model is primarily oriented toward Tier 1, there can be implementations of it that are more information system-, or Tier 3-

---

[77] In the mediated trust model, the first organization typically has no insight into the nature of the trust relationship between the second and third organizations.

[78] The authoritative organization explicitly accepts the risks to be incurred by all organizations covered by the mandate and is accountable for the risk-related decisions imposed by the organization.

oriented. An example of this application might be the use of authentication services that validate the authenticity or identity of an information system component or service.

The nature of a particular information technology service can also impact the suitability and the applicability of the various trust models. The validated trust model is the more traditional model for validating the trust of an information technology product, system, or service. However, this trust model works best in situations where there is a degree of control between parties (e.g., a contract between the government and an external service provider) or where there is sufficient time to obtain and validate the evidence needed to establish a trust relationship. Validated trust is a suboptimal model for situations where the two parties are peers and/or where the trust decisions regarding shared/supplied services must occur quickly due to the very dynamic and rapid nature of the service being requested/provided (e.g., service-oriented architectures).

APPENDIX H

RISK RESPONSE STRATEGIES
FROM BOUNDARY PROTECTION TO AGILE DEFENSES

Organizations develop *risk management strategies* as part of the risk framing step in the risk management process described in Chapter Three. The risk management strategies address how organizations intend to assess risk, respond to risk, and monitor risk—making explicit and transparent the risk perceptions that organizations routinely use in making both investment and operational decisions. As part of organizational risk management strategies, organizations also develop *risk response strategies*. The practical realities facing organizations today make risk response strategies essential—the realities of needing the mission/business effectiveness offered by information technology, the lack of trustworthiness in the technologies available, and the growing awareness by adversaries of the potential to achieve their objectives to cause harm by compromising organizational information systems and the environments in which those systems operate. Senior leaders/executives in modern organizations are faced with an almost intractable dilemma—that is, the information technologies needed for mission/business success may be the same technologies through which adversaries cause mission/business failure. The risk response strategies developed and implemented by organizations provide these senior leaders/executives (i.e., decision makers within organizations) with practical, pragmatic paths for dealing with this dilemma. Clearly defined and articulated risk response strategies help to ensure that senior leaders/executives take ownership of organizational risk responses and are ultimately *responsible* and *accountable* for risk decisions—understanding, acknowledging, and explicitly accepting the resulting mission/business risk.

As described in Chapter Two, there are five basic types of responses to risk: (i) accept; (ii) avoid; (iii) mitigate; (iv) share; and (v) transfer.[79] While each type of response can have an associated strategy, there should be an overall strategy for selecting from among the basic response types. This overall risk response strategy and a strategy for each type of response are discussed below. In addition, specific *risk mitigation strategies* are presented, including a description of how such strategies can be implemented within organizations.

H.1 OVERALL RISK RESPONSE STRATEGIES

Risk response strategies specify: (i) individuals or organizational subcomponents that are responsible for the selected risk response measures and specifications of effectiveness criteria (i.e., articulation of indicators and thresholds against which the effectiveness of risk response measures can be judged); (ii) dependencies of the selected risk response measures on other risk response measures; (iii) dependencies of selected risk response measures on other factors (e.g., implementation of other planned information technology measures); (iv) implementation timeline for risk responses; (v) plans for monitoring the effectiveness of the risk response measures; (vi) identification of risk monitoring triggers; and (vii) interim risk response measures selected for implementation, if appropriate. Risk response implementation strategies may include interim measures that organizations choose to implement. An overall risk response strategy provides an organizational approach to selecting between the basic risk responses for a given risk situation. A decision to *accept* risk must be consistent with the stated organizational tolerance for risk. Yet

---

[79] There is overlap between the basic risk responses. For example, a shared risk is one that is being accepted by each party in the sharing arrangement, and avoiding risk can be thought of as mitigating risk to zero. Nonetheless, with this understanding of overlap, there is value in addressing each of the five types of risk responses separately.

there is still need for a well-defined, established organizational path for selecting one or a combination of the risk responses of acceptance, avoidance, mitigation, sharing, or transfer. Organizations are often placed in situations where there is greater risk than the designated senior leaders/executives desire to accept. Some risk acceptance will likely be necessary. It might be possible to avoid risk or to share or transfer risk, and some risk mitigation is probably feasible. Avoiding risk may require selective reengineering of organizational mission/business processes and forgoing some of the benefits being accrued by the use of information technology organization-wide, perhaps even what organizations perceive as *necessary* benefits. Mitigating risk requires expenditure of limited resources and may quickly become cost-ineffective due to the pragmatic realities of the degree of mitigation that can actually be achieved. Lastly, risk sharing and transfer have ramifications as well, some of which if not unacceptable, may be undesirable. The risk response strategies of organizations empower senior leaders/executives to make risk-based decisions compliant with the goals, objectives, and broader organizational perspectives.

H.2 RISK ACCEPTANCE STRATEGIES

Organizational *risk acceptance strategies* are essential companions to organizational statements of risk tolerance. The objective of establishing an organizational risk tolerance is to state in clear and unambiguous terms, a limit for risk—that is, how far organizations are willing to go with regard to accepting risk to organizational operations (including missions, functions, image, and reputation), organizational assets, individuals, other organizations, and the Nation. Real-world operations, however, are seldom so simple as to make such risk tolerance statements the end-statement for risk acceptance decisions. Organizational risk acceptance strategies place the acceptance of risk into a framework of organizational perspectives on dealing with the practical realities of operating with risk and provide the guidance necessary to ensure that the extent of the risk being accepted in specific situations is compliant with organizational direction.

H.3 RISK AVOIDANCE STRATEGIES

Of all the risk response strategies, organizational *risk avoidance strategies* may be the key to achieving adequate risk response. The pragmatic realities of the trustworthiness of information technologies available for use within common resource constraints, make wise use of those technologies arguably a significant, if not *the* most significant risk response. Wise use of the information technologies that compose organizational information systems is fundamentally a form of risk avoidance—that is, organizations modify how information technologies are used to change the nature of the risk being incurred (i.e., avoid the risk). Yet such approaches can be in great tension with organizational desires and in some cases, the mandate to fully automate mission/business processes. Organizations proactively address this dilemma so that: (i) senior leaders/executives (and other organizational officials making risk-based decisions) are held accountable for only that which is within their ability to affect; and (ii) decision makers can make the difficult risk decisions that may, in fact, be in the best interests of organizations.

H.4 RISK SHARING AND TRANSFER STRATEGIES

Organizational *risk sharing strategies* and *risk transfer strategies* are key elements in enabling risk decisions for specific organizational missions/business functions at Tier 2 or organizational information systems at Tier 3. Risk sharing and transfer strategies both consider and take full advantage of a lessening of risk by sharing/transferring the potential impact across other internal organizational elements or with other external organizations—making the case that some other entities are, in fact, wholly (transfer) or partly (share) responsible and accountable for risk. For risk sharing or risk transfer to be effective risk responses, the impact on the local environment (e.g., mission/business processes or information systems) must be addressed by the sharing or transfer (i.e., the focus must be on mission/business success, not assigning blame). In addition, risk sharing and risk transfer activities must be carried out in accordance with intra- and inter-organizational dynamics and realities (e.g., organizational culture, governance, risk tolerance). This explains why risk sharing/transfer strategies are particularly important for the sharing and/or transfer to be a viable risk response option.

H.5 RISK MITIGATION STRATEGIES

Organizational *risk mitigation strategies* reflect an organizational perspective on what mitigations are to be employed and where the mitigations are to be applied, to reduce information security risks to organizational operations and assets, individuals, other organizations, and the Nation. Risk mitigation strategies are the primary link between organizational risk management programs and information security programs—with the former covering all aspects of managing risk and the latter being primarily a part of the risk response component of the risk management process. Effective *risk mitigation strategies* consider the general placement and allocation of mitigations, the degree of intended mitigation, and cover mitigations at Tier 1 (e.g., common controls), at Tier 2 (e.g., enterprise architecture including embedded information security architecture, and risk-aware mission/business processes), and at Tier 3 (security controls in individual information systems). Organizational risk mitigation strategies reflect the following:

- Mission/business processes are designed with regard to information protection needs and information security requirements;[80]

- Enterprise architectures (including embedded information security architectures) are designed with consideration for realistically achievable risk mitigations;

- Risk mitigation measures are implemented within organizational information systems and environments of operation by safeguards/countermeasure (i.e., security controls) consistent with information security architectures; and

- Information security programs, processes, and safeguards/countermeasures are highly *flexible* and *agile* with regard to implementation, recognizing the diversity in organizational missions and business functions and the dynamic environments in which the organizations operate.[81]

Organizations develop risk mitigation strategies based on strategic goals and objectives, mission and business requirements, and organizational priorities. The strategies provide the basis for making risk-based decisions on the information security solutions associated with and applied to information systems within the organization. Risk mitigation strategies are necessary to ensure that organizations are adequately protected against the growing threats to information processed, stored, and transmitted by organizational information systems. The nature of the threats and the dynamic environments in which organizations operate, demand flexible and scalable defenses as well as solutions that can be tailored to meet rapidly changing conditions. These conditions include, for example, the emergence of new threats and vulnerabilities, the development of new technologies, changes in missions/business requirements, and/or changes to environments of operation. Effective risk mitigation strategies support the goals and objectives of organizations and established mission/business priorities, are tightly coupled to enterprise architectures and information security architectures, and can operate throughout the system development life cycle.

---

[80] In addition to mission/business-driven information protection needs, information security requirements are obtained from a variety of sources (e.g., federal legislation, policies, directives, regulations, and standards).

[81] Dynamic environments of operation are characterized, for example, by ongoing changes in people, processes, technologies, physical infrastructure, and threats.

Traditional risk mitigation strategies with regard to threats from cyber attacks at first relied almost exclusively on monolithic *boundary protection*. These strategies assumed adversaries were outside of some established defensive perimeter, and the objective of organizations was to repel the attack. The primary focus of static boundary protection was penetration resistance of the information technology products and information systems employed by the organization as well as any additional safeguards and countermeasures implemented in the environments in which the products and systems operated. Recognition that information system boundaries were permeable or porous led to defense-in-depth as part of the mitigation strategy, relying on detection and response mechanisms to address the threats within the protection perimeter. In today's world characterized by *advanced persistent threats*,[82] a more comprehensive risk mitigation strategy is needed—a strategy that combines traditional boundary protection with *agile defense.*

Agile defense assumes that a small percentage of threats from purposeful cyber attacks will be successful by compromising organizational information systems through the supply chain[83] by defeating the initial safeguards and countermeasures (i.e., security controls) implemented by organizations, or by exploiting previously unidentified vulnerabilities for which protections are not in place. In this scenario, adversaries are operating inside the defensive perimeters established by organizations and may have substantial or complete control of organizational information systems. Agile defense employs the concept of *information system resilience*—that is, the ability of systems to operate while under attack, even in a degraded or debilitated state, and to rapidly recover operational capabilities for essential functions after a successful attack. The concept of information system resilience can also be applied to the other classes of threats including threats from environmental disruptions and/or human errors of omission/commission. The most effective risk mitigation strategies employ a combination of boundary protection and agile defenses depending on the characteristics of the threat.[84] This dual protection strategy illustrates two important information security concepts known as defense-in-depth[85] and defense-in-breadth.[86]

> *Information has value and must be protected. Information systems (including people, processes, and technologies) are the primary vehicles employed to process, store, and transmit such information— allowing organizations to carry out their missions in a variety of environments of operation and to ultimately be successful.*

---

[82] An *advanced persistent threat* is an adversary that possesses sophisticated levels of expertise and significant resources which allow it to create opportunities to achieve its objectives by using multiple attack vectors (e.g., cyber, physical, and deception). These objectives typically include establishing/extending footholds within the information technology infrastructure of the targeted organizations for purposes of exfiltrating information, undermining or impeding critical aspects of a mission, program, or organization; or positioning itself to carry out these objectives in the future. The advanced persistent threat: (i) pursues its objectives repeatedly over an extended period of time; (ii) adapts to defenders' efforts to resist it; and (iii) is determined to maintain the level of interaction needed to execute its objectives.

[83] Draft NIST Interagency Report 7622 provides guidance on managing supply chain risk.

[84] Threat characteristics include capabilities, intentions, and targeting information.

[85] *Defense-in-depth* is an information security strategy integrating people, technology, and operations capabilities to establish variable barriers across multiple layers and missions of the organization.

[86] *Defense-in-breadth* is a planned, systematic set of multidisciplinary activities that seek to identify, manage, and reduce risk of exploitable vulnerabilities at every stage of the system, network, or subcomponent life cycle (system, network, or product design and development; manufacturing; packaging; assembly; system integration; distribution; operations; maintenance; and retirement).

www.ingramcontent.com/pod-product-compliance
Lightning Source LLC
Chambersburg PA
CBHW060202060326
40690CB00018B/4219